Bob,

I value your friendship. Please accept this complimentary copy of my book as an expression of my appreciation.

All the best...

Millie

12-10-07

ENTERING THE PROMISED LAND
Published by
Entering The Promised Land GP, LLC
P.O. Box 926215
Houston, TX   77292-6215

For information about bulk purchases, please contact:
www.enteringthepromisedland.com

ENTERING THE PROMISED LAND

Cover design by Gilbreath Communications, Inc.
Tracy L. Price, Senior Art Director

Dust Jacket Photo of Willie J. Alexander by
Alexander's Fine Portrait Design

Publishing Consultant: Marsha Tucker
Editor: Wayne Hall

Printed in the United States of America

1 3 5 7 9 10 8 6 4 2

Library of Congress Cataloging-in-Publication Data has been applied for.

ISBN-13: 978-0-9798779-0-2
ISBN-10: 0-9798779-0-3

Dedication

I am truly a blessed man to have the love of my wife, Carolyn, and our children, Michael and Alexis. Carolyn, thank you for loving me these many years. And Michael and Alexis for being the best son and daughter a dad can have. Without your support, I could not have done this. I dedicate Entering the Promised Land *to you.*

Preface

Sometimes what occurs in life is beyond comprehension! When I reflect on how I've had to approach writing this book, a couple of old sayings spring to mind: "You can't fit a square peg in a round hole," and, "It is neither fish nor fowl." Or, better yet, in the words of baseball great Yogi Berra, when you come to a fork in the road you, "take it!" Note that Yogi doesn't advise which fork to take. That's exactly the dilemma that confronted me while writing *Entering the Promised Land*. My advisors and I struggled with trying to categorize this book. When it was finished, I was told that it was two different books. I needed to decide whether it would be about business or religion, and that I shouldn't mix the two. I was told the reader would begin reading a fascinating secular story that most black business people and black people in general could relate to and understand. However, the book then abruptly turns and takes the reader on a biblical journey. This abrupt turn, I was told, could confuse the reader.

My response is that this book is about a personal journey. The way it is written was how it was revealed. Why can't the book deal with both secular and biblical issues? Both are at the heart of black people's problems. Just because something has always been done a certain way, doesn't mean it can't be changed. After all, this book is different. It's a serious writing, a true story, autobiographical and divinely inspired. It is divine inspiration as summed up best by Sister Speranza, a contemporary mystic and founder of the sanctuary of "The Most Merciful Love." She is quoted in the *Diary of Saint Maria Faustina Kowalska, — Divine Mercy in My Soul.*[1]

When asked what she thought of Sister Maria Faustina's writings, Sister Speranza commented: "The writings contain a wonderful teaching, but reading them one must remember that God speaks to philosophers in the language of philosophers and to simple souls in the language of the simple ones, and only to these last does He reveal truths hidden from the wise and prudent of this world."

The issues dealt with in this book, just like my life or yours, are too complex to explain with a simple story. Life in general does not allow one to categorize it into one finite point or moment. There are good and bad, happy and sad, prosperous and poverty-stricken times. A person cannot describe his life with accurate detail without including a beginning, middle and end, both secular and biblical references.

As a child and adolescent, the first part of my life was lived around and near poverty. The second part of my life as a professional football player was lived in prosperity. The third part of my life as a businessman and community volunteer has been a combination of the two. It was the confluence of the two that caused the internal conflict and led to the eventual writing of this book.

During a typical work day, it is common for me to be in palatial surroundings for a business breakfast meeting. Hours later, I might meet with a minister and listen to his comments about his congregation thinking his $1,000 a month salary is too much, or a civic group trying to raise (what seems to be a massive amount of) money to buy books and install updated computer technology for their local library. I have worked on a fund-raising event that effortlessly raised over a half million dollars, then turned around to work on a fund-raiser in the black community where we struggled to raise $60,000. I may add that both efforts were needed and of equal importance to their respective communities.

Entering the Promised Land begins in 1956 at the time of the Montgomery [Alabama] Bus Boycott. Parts of the story that are omitted occurred in the middle of my life. While that part of my life was important, the importance was not necessarily germane to the story. What is germane is that on December 4, 2002, something prompted me to stand before a powerful business group in downtown Houston and deliver an impromptu state of the union message about black Houstonians.

After that speech, I was overcome with fear for having been so outspoken and prayed to God for help and to find an inner peace that had eluded me. That help came in the form of what I call divine intervention from God: meeting people before and during the writing of this book who would provide assistance and the gathering of research information that appeared to be literally thrown in front of me. In fact, the research information came to me so easily and in such a way that I couldn't miss it. To miss it, I would have literally had to walk around it!

What started out as delving into black people's business is-sues, quickly developed into biblical reading and study. I went on a journey that took me from the secular, to the biblical, back to the secular. My journey led me to research from current times back to the Civil Rights Movement, to ancient Egypt, to the Promised Land, across the Sahara Desert, to the west coast of Africa, across the Atlantic Ocean, to Jamestown, Virginia and plantations in the South, back to the Civil Rights Movement and then back to modern-day.

My research gained new momentum after I read a copy of Dr. Martin Luther King's 1968 speech, "I See the Promised Land." While reading the speech, I was amazed at the broad scope of subjects Dr. King addressed and the intensity of his words. Much of what he said is still quite relevant to black people's lives today. As I was writing this book, I would tell people about my book and about Dr. King's speech. Invariably, they would ask me to e-mail them a copy of the 1968 speech. I would e-mail the speech and never hear any more about it.

For me, there was no turning back as the path was clear. The more I read the speech and read the Bible, I knew the answers to black people's economic problems were in the Bible. As I started my reading, I quickly saw the parallel between the prophet Moses and Dr. Martin Luther King. Moses led the children of Israel out of Egypt (and their subsequent camping at Mount Sinai). Dr. Martin Luther King, Jr. led the Civil Rights Movement which brought about the signing of the Civil Rights Act in 1964.

Attending church one Sunday revealed how the modern-day image of Jesus Christ was conceived. I came to understand how this image may have and continue to contribute to the lack of dignity in black people today. This lack of dignity impacts the way black people think and why other ethnic groups may view black people in a nega-tive way.

Conducting research in *The Oxford English Dictionary* led to the discovery of a book titled, *The Travels of Sir John Mandeville.* I would learn that historians have speculated that "John Mandeville" is simply the pen name of an author who presented the writings of others as his own. However, historians have never discredited the actual information presented in Mandeville's book.

In Mandeville's book, several biblical references led me to take a second look at the Bible with particular interest in the family of

Abraham, God's chosen people. I now believe that some African-descended people were and are descendants of Abraham.

In parts of this book where descriptive biblical detail is used, I alert and remind the reader that the Bible is written in metaphoric language. Words, on their surface, often have meanings that are not always evident. For example, I contend that the term "serpent" as used in the book of Genesis is a metaphor for a man who seduces Eve.

Using what I describe as a new approach for translating biblical scripture, I discovered what I believe is the place of man's origin. The approach further reveals the culture and skin color of the first man on earth. These discoveries are significant as they unlock the lost history of black people living in America who are descendants of slaves.

Entering the Promised Land attempts to understand the financial struggles of black people. United States citizens live in the richest country in the world, yet two-thirds of the black citizens live either at near-poverty or at poverty levels that rivals inhabitants living in a third world country.

In his book, *Ike's Final Battle — The Road to Little Rock and the Challenge of Equality*, Kasey S. Pipes writes, "Historians, like archaeologists, often search for the Rosetta Stone. Something new, different, earth-shattering; a code that will unlock history's hidden treasures." [2]

I believe *Entering the Promised Land* is the Rosetta Stone that unlocks the history of black people in America. This book is about deciphering the true meaning of words as they relate to the history of black people. Once you have read this transcript, perhaps more than once, you will have what I believe is a true sense of black people's heritage and history. This book should stimulate your thinking and reasoning about the history and how it transcends time and relates to our present day.

Willie J. Alexander
August 3, 2007
Houston, Texas

Contents

Prologue

A major inspiration for writing this book is my belief that a broad-based assault on the self-image of African-Americans has persisted for too long. Harsh assessments about the present and future state of African-Americans can be heard from all corners.

It is commonplace for both white and black middle-class Americans to blame the worst of society's ills exclusively on the urban black community — individuals who live in the so-called "ghetto." For example, many attribute drug abuse and drug-related violent crime almost exclusively to young black males. Drug abuse has always been and continues to be quite high among all racial and ethnic groups.

This troubling reality is highlighted by the National Institute on Drug Abuse in its 2005 nationwide study, Monitoring the Future, that "Current and lifetime use of illicit drugs was lower for black 8th, 10th and 12th graders than white and Hispanic students. Among 12th graders, whites tended to have the highest rates of lifetime use for a number of drugs. Hispanics generally have rates of use for many drugs that tend to fall between that of whites and blacks. However, Hispanics have the highest rate of lifetime usage for crack, heroin, Rohypnol and crystal methamphetamine.[3]

Despite documented facts like these, many take their uninformed opinions from profit-driven films, trashy television dramas or questionable evening "news" reports. Let's face it, the media plays a significant role in how we identify people. And in many cases the reports are made in such a nonchalant manor that the inaccuracies are easily taken as fact. For example, rarely are assertions about "black drug use," "black laziness" and "black crime" based on real evidence and documented facts. If we did any research, we would quickly find that the facts often disprove the ugly stereotypes we so easily accept.

Writing this book has been an educational and liberating process for me, personally. I started writing with a deep sense of anger and frustration. By the time I finished, I had acquired a new sense of calm and determination to face daily challenges. My prayer is that the same will happen for you.

For those who believe in God, may this book deepen your faith. For scholars who maintain or defend certain dogma about the Bible, may this book offer a chance to re-examine old assumptions. For those who have questions about both the secular and the religious worlds, may it answer your deepest questions. And may this book spur nonbelievers to take another look at the Bible and what it teaches!

This book is not meant to exclude non-black readers; rather it is an attempt to encourage understanding and dialogue among all races and religions. It is also an attempt to encourage everyone — *including black people themselves* — to cultivate true respect and admiration for the long and turbulent history of African-descended peoples and their struggle against extreme adversity.

But I intend to address black people first and foremost. Especially young blacks, many of whom may be experiencing the

same anger and frustration I once felt. I want black youths growing up today — and the unborn black children who may read this
book many years from now — to take away this message: "You
have to like yourself to fend off the hostility and prejudgment of
others. You are a special person. You have a very rich and proud
heritage. Your ancestral line, as those of all men and women, goes
directly to Adam and Eve — and as my research finds — back
through Jesus Christ. In spite of all the obstacles your ancestors
overcame, despite the obstacles you face today and will likely
face tomorrow, only you can stop you from being successful. And
only you can ensure your life will reach its full potential and purpose."

It is crucial to stop and reflect on the 1,800 years of missing
African history, African-American struggle against slavery; and the
legalized oppression of the Jim Crow era. In spite of such brutal
adversity, black men and women survived and sustained themselves through a sense of self-worth — and a strong faith in God's
promise of deliverance.

Always remember your history is filled with people of self-
reliance, ingenuity and greatness. You must learn about men like
Noah, the shipbuilder (Genesis 6:14-16); Jubal, the first musi-
cian-inventor of the harp and flute (Genesis 4:21); Tubal-cain, the
first to work with metal, forging instruments of bronze and iron
(Genesis 4:22); Nimrod, a great hunter, heroic warrior and a builder
of empires (Genesis 10:8-12).

In short, you must learn that your history is much deeper
and broader than what has been promoted by today's mass media. Some of the greatest black role models were never featured

on magazine covers or in television interviews. Take note of the countless numbers of black men and women around the world who rose against all odds to become sport legends, creators of fine art, successful business leaders or dedicated and effective civic or political leaders.

African-Americans throughout history stand as everlasting examples of how to survive and overcome overwhelming obstacles. This will become evident as you walk with me on a journey that begins with a walk in a world of giants and then sorts out our past to show the biblical ancestry of blacks, which lays the groundwork for a more prosperous black future in America. After reading this book it is my hope that the reader will agree, the best is yet to come and that African-Americans will once again enter the Promised Land.

Chapter 1 - A Speech to the Giants

Montgomery, Alabama 1956 — It was bill-paying day. Mother Dear had me in tow, walking to town on what the weatherman would describe as a chilly, overcast fall day. We were on foot because of the bus boycott; Rosa Parks had recently made history by refusing to move to the back of the bus. Walking was nothing new to Mother Dear. As newlyweds, she and my dad had walked most of the way to Montgomery from Lowndes County, Alabama, their birthplace.

My parents did not have a bank account. Most black people didn't. Bills were paid with cash, in person and on Saturday. I was excited to be on this important mission and even more excited that Mother Dear let me stand alone on the sidewalk outside the utility company while she took care of business inside. It was a clear demonstration of her trust.

I waited, a seven-year-old pretty full of himself. A white boy, a little older and larger, approached from down the sidewalk. Looming over me, he got in my face and said in a nasty and intimidating voice, "What are you doing standing here, nigger?"

Terrified, I froze against the storefront. A string of foul words poured from him; it seemed they poured all over me. Then he walked away. Tears welled and spilled down my cheeks just as Mother Dear came outside. "Willie James," she asked, concerned, "what's wrong with you, boy?" In a voice choked with tears I told her that a white boy had called me "nigger."

Mother Dear hugged me close. "Willie James don't you pay that boy no mind," she said. "You always remember: you are going to run across bad white folks in life and good white folks. You are going to run across bad colored folks in life and good colored folks. You remember to judge people for who they are."

Almost a decade later, the nation would hear a young Dr. Martin Luther King, Jr. on the steps of the Lincoln Memorial say, "I have a dream that my four children will one day live in a nation where they will not be judged by the color of their skin but by the content of their character." On this subject, Dr. King and my mother shared the same outlook: You remember to judge people for who they are.

****

On a bright, sunny morning early in December 2002, I left a client meeting on Houston's East End to drive downtown for a Greater Houston Partnership Board of Directors meeting. Armed with a copy of the July 2001 issue of *Black Enterprise*,[4] thoughts of the black business development efforts currently under way in Houston weighed heavily on my mind. Little did I know this month would be one of great revelation.

As I drove down Interstate 10 en route to the meeting, my thoughts were racing. I kept thinking it was the last meeting I would attend because my term on the board was coming to an end and it would be the last chance to raise the black economic issue.

The Greater Houston Partnership was created to further

the economic development of Houston. It is the city's chief lobbying entity and business promoter. Its mission statement says that it seeks to make Houston a better place in which to live, work and to do business. The membership is comprised of business people from throughout the Houston area, although its primary membership is principally the corporations headquartered downtown, such as ExxonMobil, Continental Airlines and the now–defunct Enron Corp.

I joined the Partnership Board in 1994. My company, W.J. Alexander & Associates, P.C., is an employee benefits consulting and insurance brokerage services firm which has provided services for several other Partnership members.

The Partnership's Board meeting generally is a gathering of Houston's powerbrokers along with the few minority members like me who are deemed sufficient in number to make its composition "diverse." It is an august body, where power and influence sit at the conference table. In biblical times, they would have been the giants inhabiting the Promised Land (Numbers 13:33).

I was also thinking about an article I had read in that July 2001 issue of *Black Enterprise*. The article had declared Houston the best city for African-Americans to live and, presumably, to do business. The U.S. Census Bureau and Department of Labor statistics reported in the article — by my math — painted a pretty dismal economic picture for African-Americans. I thought: "My God, if Houston is the best place for black people to live — from an economic standpoint — the rest of the country is in really dire shape."

A few minutes before the Board meeting convened, I vis-

ited with another member — a very nice and a very wealthy gentleman. While I was friends with many on the board, I did not know
this particular board member personally. But he was always re-
spectful and friendly toward me. His legacy in business, like the
other board members, reflects that he had worked hard to become successful and desired to make Houston a better place to
live. Our conversation became personal and he shared with me
that he and his wife came to Houston in 1949 with everything they
owned in their automobile.

While I listened, my thoughts turned to my dad and how different
his life had been. He and my mother left Lowndes County, Alabama in
1939 and virtually walked to Montgomery with everything they owned on
their backs. Fortunately, shortly after arriving in Montgomery, my dad
was able to get a job working on the railroad.

The meeting's agenda called for the board's incoming chairperson (the first woman to serve in this position) to give the strategic and
operating plan for the next year. As I listened to her report, I waited for
her to talk about minority business issues. The Partnership has numerous
committees working on a variety of issues impacting Houston — from
flood control to health care delivery to air quality. I felt certain some part
of the plan would include minority business issues, as all year long there
had been much discussion about these issues and how the Partnership
could play a role.

The incoming chairperson concluded her presentation with no
mention of minority business issues. The good book says there's a time
for everything, "There is a time to be quiet and a time to speak up." As the
meeting drew to a close, I asked the outgoing chairman if I could address
the Board. I stood before Houston's prominent white business leaders

and other minority business people, including the few African-Americans on the Board with my knees shaking and my mouth dry.

As I write this now and reflect on the extemporaneous speech that transpired, I want to express my deep respect and gratitude to the Board members and the chairman who graciously gave me the opportunity to express my thoughts and feelings in a way that even I had not anticipated. I am aware that the chairman or other board members chose to hear me out even though many of them may have been uncomfortable with my speech.

I remember telling the other members that I wanted to talk to them about three issues that affect the African-American community: jobs and career growth in those jobs, contracting opportunities for businesses and funding for not-for-profits. I did not want to speak on minority business issues in general as I could not communicate about them. I could not get my arms around the problems facing other minorities, but I could speak to them as an African-American.

I started my speech by holding up the copy of *Black Enterprise* and pointing out that on the cover were two prominent Houstonians. I told them about the article citing Houston as the number one city for African-Americans and I reminded them that in 2001, the Partnership chairman at that time had made note of this very article at one of the Board meetings.

As I made eye contact with my fellow Board members, I noticed the incredulous expression on the faces of my African-American counterparts. I also noticed that the white board members were equally surprised as their glances toward one another seemed to bounce around the room.

Of course, that made me even more nervous. It was like the old expression about the elephant in the room no one talks about — and if anybody dares to mention it, everyone is uncomfortable. But I knew deep down that what I had to say needed to be said. I quoted to them from the magazine article an *Entrepreneurship Opportunities Matrix* — which listed the total number of black businesses in Houston, the total number of black employees and the total revenues of all black businesses.

The sources cited by the article were the 1997 U.S. Census Bureau data and the Department of Labor.[5] In Houston, the article reported, there were 16,855 black-owned businesses with 22,409 employees and annual sales of $1.4 billion.

By my math, each black-owned business employed an average of 1.3 employees and had average annual sales of only $84,000. This is the best city in the entire country for black people! Shortly after my speech to the GHP Board, I learned an article in the Houston Chronicle dated July 13, 2001,[6] stated the average Houston minority-owned business earned $333,487 in 1997 according to the U.S. Department of Commerce. One might say that without African-American annual sales, the $333,487 for minority businesses would be higher. "When I dissect these numbers," I said, "I realize that as an African-American businessman, I cannot even hope to do business with Houston's African-American community — not with the service offerings of my company. And that, my friends, is why I come to you to do business."

I was on a roll now and continued: "But what happens when I — a black businessman — come to you to do business? And I have called on many of you in this room. You honor me with a meeting, which I appreciate. During our appointment, I share with you the service offerings of W.J. Alexander & Associates and also share with you the names of several clients. Many times after my presentation, I believe there is a genuine interest by you for your company to do business with my firm. What follows our meeting is a one-on-one meeting with that individual and a series of meetings with other staffers, and almost every time, no genuine business relationship is developed. After the fact, I realize that I probably got a miscue — that your interest in me was personal, not professional.

"I want you to understand that I was born and raised in Montgomery, Alabama during the height of the Civil Rights Movement. Back then, I knew where I stood with white folks. I stayed on my side of town; they stayed on their side of town."

"So when I walk away from one of these arranged meetings without even a glimmer of a hope of having your business, these are the thoughts running through my mind: Is it because there is a relationship in place where there are very good services and as a result I cannot penetrate the relationship? Was it because they thought that my firm, W.J. Alexander & Associates, did not have the skill sets in order to provide the services the company needs; or is it because I am black?"

"It is time for us to talk about racism. I call on my fellow black board members to say that it is time for us to share with this body the conversations that we have about these very issues in our private time. It is time for us to talk about it because in our world, the world of black folks, we believe it exists. I do not know whether in your world you feel that racism still exists, but let me share a few observations with you."

"I am a people-watcher, especially when I am in downtown Houston calling on your businesses. From my vantage point, I have made a very crude and random sampling of black employment in downtown.

Based on what I see, I would estimate that in corporate Houston today, only 2 percent to 3 percent of the workforce is black." (Note: Since my speech in 2002, I've seen statistics in a report from the U.S. Equal Employment Opportunity Commission: Job Patterns for Minorities and Women in Private Industry. The report indicates the actual nationwide statistic in 2005 for black people in the U.S. workforce comprise 7.3% of the overall workforce[7].) In this case, perception was not too far from reality.

"I do not deny that blacks have jobs, but they are not corporate jobs. Black people work for the U.S. Postal Service, Houston Independent School District and for other governmental entities. They are in service positions; that is, they are the cooks in the kitchens and the janitors and maintenance crews in the basements of businesses, schools and hospitals."

"Corporate America has given a select few African-Americans the opportunity for advancement. I applaud CenterPoint Energy for naming an African-American as chairman of the board. On the other hand, I challenge anyone in this room to show me anywhere in a major Houston corporation where more than one black person, at any give time, works in an executive leadership position. As a matter of fact, even as you go down into the next tier, I challenge you to show me where there is more than one black person working in senior level management. And I reiterate that these employees are the best and the brightest African-Americans. It is time to start putting our best and our brightest students from our universities on a track to get to the top of your corporations. But what about the average African-American? When will it be time to give them a chance to work inside corporate America? Now is the time!"

The next issue I raised was the comparative lack of support for African-American charities. I shared with the board that for many years, I had volunteered for several of the city's major charities and raised funds for them. I also had raised money for the United Negro College Fund and for the past three years chaired a prominent African-American annual fund-raising event. "What I have noticed in fund-raising," I said, "is that the average major gift by corporations to black not-for-profits is $5,000, whereas white charities receive many times that amount."

By this time, my nervousness and dry mouth were noticeable and the president of the Partnership offered me a glass of water. Why wouldn't I be nervous with a dry mouth? I was dealing with topics that — to my knowledge — had never been discussed in the public domain, and definitely not in this forum.

I ended and thanked everyone for listening. I stood behind the podium, waiting for who knows what — questions, the opening of a dialogue. Were they shocked? Angered? Could they not digest the truth? Or did words fail them? I thought for God's sake, say something. The silence was deafening. As my dad would have said, "You could have heard a rat pissin' on cotton."

Finally, another African-American stood up. He said to the

group: "I want you to know that I agree with everything that Willie has said. Let me explain to you about his comments on fund-raising. How is it that this city's corporations will give $5,000 as a large gift to an African-American not-for-profit dealing with human needs, then turn around and give $100,000 to the Symphony?"

A very prominent corporate leader, in his last Partnership meeting, also stood up and said: "I want you to recall that I tried to address this issue when I was chairman of the Partnership, and that it died for lack of support from this body."

After the meeting adjourned, several board members made various comments to me like: "Wow, Willie, I really didn't know it was like that" and, "You know, Willie, some white folks think that Jim Crow is dead." And another board member said, "Give me a call later. I'd like to explore that topic with you further and share some of my ideas." He and I did talk later and the product of that lengthy conversation was an agreement that we would begin developing a plan to address African-American economic empowerment. On December 13, 2002, I received an e-mail from him. His e-mail talked about the next step. Even though this very powerful and influential gentleman had made offers to help, past history reminded me that I needed to explore solutions on my own. I had made a bold statement to the Partnership and doing so demanded that I follow up with action.

Surprisingly, before any action, my speech attracted the interest of what would become two new W.J. Alexander & Associates' business clients. Another interest led to a meeting with a CEO who introduced me to one of his subordinates. The contact with this person was unproductive — which was the kind of run-around I had dealt with for years.

Immediately following the speech to the Greater Houston Partnership I was very conflicted. In my heart, I had no regrets for the truth of what I said. But, to be honest, I was very worried about the possible fallout. After all, despite my criticism of the lack of opportunity for African-Americans, I had achieved a degree of success relative to other African-Americans, even though my success was not what it could have been if I were white.

As a high school athlete, college All-American football player and a professional football player for almost a decade, I knew success. It was only after I left professional football to enter the business world that I came to a startling realization. I found there was a huge difference between wanting something I was going to get anyway and desiring something more than my lot in life had set out for me. The first requires only patience, the latter, determination.

My earlier success opened doors, usually because someone wanted to talk sports with the former Houston Oilers' Number 19. Doing business was another matter and there were limits to how far I could go. In the corporate world, if lucky, I might get some business after months, even years, of repeated calls. The energy fueling my eagerness and dreams when I entered the business world was now fueling total frustration at the moment when I stood before the corporate giants.

My frustration felt justified when almost five years later in 2007, I discovered that, according to recent figures published by the U.S. Census Bureau[8], revenues of black businesses in Houston had decreased since the last published 1997 Economic Census report. The report showed average annual revenues for black businesses had plummeted from $84,000 to $74,000. The average number of employees for black businesses dropped from 1.3 per business to .96 — less than one employee per business, which means many are functioning as a one-person operation. As dismal as these numbers appear, they get worse.

Stunningly, the 2006 report also reveals only 1,374 black businesses had paid employees in Houston, a significant decrease from the 21,226 total numbers of black businesses. To drive home the message — 19,852 of the 21,226 total black businesses in Houston did not have any paid employees other than the owner. Not surprisingly, the 1,374 black businesses with paid employees generated a disproportionate 1.1 billion dollars of the total 1.562 billion dollars generated by all black businesses. The 1.1 billion dollars generated by the 1,374 black businesses provided an average annual revenue base of $800,582 for black businesses with paid employees. These black businesses represented six percent of all black businesses in Houston and accounted for 70% of the total revenues generated by black businesses.

One needs to know how to look beneath the surface numbers. The fact is, a very small number of the 1,374 black businesses with employees earn above $800,582 in revenues per year. If this small number of successful black businesses did not exist, the average annual revenue base for the remaining black businesses with employees would plummet far below the stated average of $800,582.

The financially strapped black business community directly impacts the wealth or the lack thereof in the black community as a whole. Quite obviously, one-person businesses cannot help their communities because they cannot afford other employees.

I would discover in an August 31, 2006 Houston Chronicle editorial titled, "Grim facts,"[9] that "A full 29 percent of black families here [in Houston] were impoverished, a jump from 25 percent in 2000." That amounts to a 16 percent increase. In other words, economic indicators showed the city's African American community getting poorer and the numbers of African Americans in poverty were growing.

I pose this question; if Houston is the best U.S. city for black people, how much worse can it be for blacks in other U.S. cities?

One can surmise that if a business community on life support and an increasing poverty rate were across-the-board problems for all ethnic communities, government and media attention to this problem would have been far greater. I have no doubt that multiple strategy sessions would have occurred and this would have been the lead story on the television news broadcasts and on the front pages of newspapers nationwide.

Because of statistics like these, when calling on some of my black brothers and sisters for business, I could almost feel the heat on a hot check the moment it crossed my palm. I realize, to put it bluntly, that black folks ain't got no money. Isn't it ironic that in the aftermath of the black community supposedly being integrated into the overall U.S. society, black people's economic problems have gotten notably worse?

Dr. Claud Anderson talked about this phenomenon in his 2001 book, *PowerNomics,* when he noted that certain contemporary economic issues strongly resemble the dire situation blacks faced before the start of the Civil War 140 years ago. "We are '100 percent' free, yet black Americans still own only one-half of one percent of this nation's wealth. Today, the income of blacks as compared to whites has regressed to the level it was at the end of the 1960s. Approximately 38 percent of the black population is beneath the poverty line and another one-third is marginal, just above the poverty line." [10]

Almost a year later, I wrote "The Parallel" chapter in this book and discussed it with a local rabbi. After hearing it, he said the "German Jews came here (to the United States of America) in the first half of the 19th century and the Russian Jews came in the last decades of that century (1880's-1890's and early 1900's);" the wealthy German Jews snubbed their noses at the poor Russian Jews. The wealthy Jews soon came to learn that they could not elevate themselves without finding a way to elevate the poor Jews." I believe this is a lesson blacks would do well to learn. The rabbi also suggested that I purchase the book about Dr. Martin Luther King, Jr., *Bearing the Cross*, [11] by David Garrow.

When I reflect on my experience of walking in protest with my mother and over 50 years later confronting continued economic and social disparities of African-Americans, I am perplexed — why is it that in a free society both visible and invisible barriers to fairness persists? Mother Dear's lifelong lesson — You remember, to judge people for who they are — did not seem to apply to me and my people. Had I lost my faith? No! Had I lost my way? No! Through prayer, I felt that I had taken an important step that would strengthen my faith and lead me on a journey to a higher understanding.

****

At the time this book was written, five years had passed since the speech to my fellow Greater Houston Partnership board members. I had thought about that speech almost every day. The one thing that I regret not telling my fellow board members was what fueled my frustration and anger; frustration and anger that was fueled by being with the powerful and feeling so powerless.

When I started out in business, I knew that other than as a pro football player, Willie Alexander was an unknown commodity. The first item on my agenda was to make that a non-issue. I strategically developed a plan to remedy the lack of civic name identification. I decided to get involved personally in the city of Houston to make it a better place for all to live. I volunteered countless hours charitably, civically, and politically.

When I eventually reached the point where I was deemed worthy to sit in the boardroom and govern, I rolled up my sleeves and worked alongside other fellow board members to improve the charitable organization we served. When the time came to work on an event to make the city a better place to live, again, I rolled up my sleeves to work alongside other volunteers. When it came time to support good governance, I rolled up my sleeves alongside other volunteers. Willie Alexander did not seek a handout; I sought an opportunity to show my fellow board members, who were all white, that I had something to offer Houston.

If I had the time on December 4, 2002, when I spoke to my fellow board members, this is what I would have identified as the source of my frustration and anger. When calling on their companies, my key staff member(s) and I met with their corporate staff, made our presentation, and asked for an opportunity to provide our service offerings and insurance products for their company. We told them, just like with our other corporate clients: W.J. Alexander & Associates desires to get our foot in the door. We felt confident that with a small opportunity, we could grow the relationship, just as we had done with our other clients. I knew that like the camel that managed to get its nose under the tent and the rest of the body followed, if given a small project, W.J. Alexander & Associates would grow the relationship. It's not bragging when you have a proven track record with clients.

When calling on any prospect, I always remember starting out many years ago in 1980. Back then, I once heard the legendary football coach Lou Holtz say, "The only place you start at the top is digging a hole." I was age 58 at the time this book was written. After 27 years, I think that when comparing myself to my white peers, I am still "starting at the top digging a hole."

As a way to establish credibility with a prospect, we shared the name of our clients similar in size along with contact information. This information was provided for them to call and verify the quality of W.J. Alexander & Associates' work. After our presentation, I followed-up, sometimes for years and no business relationship ever developed. As the saying goes, "Every now and then, even a blind hog, can find an acorn."

Chapter 2 - The Parallel

My parents, Johnny Mack and Nellie Lee Alexander, lived in a small, neatly kept A-frame wood home built on brick pillars. The Montgomery, Alabama street we lived on was named South Lincoln Terrace. I jokingly describe our family as upper-class poor people, because Daddy owned a used automobile. He bought the car at a discounted sales price, which meant that it had motor or transmission problems. His children did the step-and-fetch to help with repairs that put the car in good working condition.

The five sons and one daughter in the Alexander household were baptized and literally raised in the Baptist church. Sunday was a holy day of obligation. At an early age and throughout my childhood, we were taught to fear God.

Easter Sunday was always a special occasion. We looked forward to the new clothes purchased from selected downtown merchants. These merchants were the only ones to give colored people credit. After church on Easter, Daddy would take the family to Freeman's Studio to take a family photograph. Oddly, Mother Dear never took a picture with us.

I was especially disappointed one Easter as the soles on my new shoes were flapping by the end of day. Imagine how Mother Dear and Daddy felt! The shoes were paid for over many months by a payment purchase plan called "layaway." Even though the shoes were obviously defective, they could not or did not have the courage to take them back to the Montgomery merchant.

I remember Mother Dear and her cousin, Essie B [Brown], and other older black adults often saying they looked forward to "going home." They believed a better life waited for them in heaven, or as some would call it, the afterlife. As an adult, I realize why they said this — life for them was a constant struggle trying to raise children and pay the bills. It was during this time when I first heard the words "making ends meet." Raising a family, while rewarding, was hard. To withstand these daily hardships, they gave their lives to the Lord.

****

In the days that followed my speech to the Greater Houston Partnership, I shared my thoughts with a friend. Of course, the subject was economic empowerment. My friend said that my speech echoed Dr. Martin Luther King's speech, "I See the Promised Land" as it appears in *A Testament of Hope – The Essential Writings and Speeches of Martin Luther King, Jr.*[12] My friend went on to say that on April 3, 1968, Dr. King gave his last known recorded remarks in Memphis, Tennessee while there supporting the garbage worker's strike. Our conversation ended with my friend promising to e-mail the speech to me.

When I received the speech, I read it repeatedly and became fascinated with Dr. King's every word. I desperately tried to understand his message. What was he saying in his last public speech when he made reference to the Pharaoh, Amos, long white robes over yonder, strengthening black institutions, boycotting

Coca-Cola and "I have been to the mountaintop?" As I read the speech, I began to wonder whether Dr. King believed history was repeating itself. Just like the children of Israel who were slaves in Egypt for 400 years, African-Americans had gone through 244 years of slavery and 100 years of Jim Crow in the United States. Looking back, the Civil Rights Movement and the signing of the Civil Rights Act was like the children of Israel when they camped at the foot of Mount Sinai. In both cases, these groups were adjusting to recently attained partial freedom.

One other striking similarity between these two groups is that they suffered because they did not have a clear sense of their identity. In the case of the Israelites, they did not have the Bible when they fled bondage. In the case of African-Americans their identity was defined largely by others. On any given day, for example, the mainstream media would paint blacks as either noble or savage. And the realities of the legacy of oppression left blacks in a situation of dependency having labor, not financial or real wealth, as their principal currency in our market-based economy.

One morning a couple of months later, I met with a pastor of a local black congregation and told him that I had been reading Dr. King's speech, "I See the Promised Land." I remember telling him, that I didn't know that on the night before Dr. King's assassination he had instructed black people to boycott Coca-Cola. I remember the pastor's words, "Let me talk to you." I spent about two hours with him that morning as he told me the story of the Bible's book of Exodus. It all ended abruptly as he had to leave for a noon appointment. I literally begged him to let me come back that afternoon. He told me to return around 3 p.m.

and he would continue his lecture.

That evening, I started my Bible reading with the book of Exodus and that's when I realized I was on a journey unlike anything I had previously experienced in my life. Through repeated and concurrent reading of the designated books of the Bible and Dr. King's speech, "I See the Promised Land," it was being revealed to me that Dr. King may have known that his role as a civil rights leader paralleled that of Moses leading the children of Israel out of Egypt.

* * * * * * * * * *

After 400 years of captivity in Egypt, God instructed the children of Israel to leave Egypt and enter the Promised Land, a land flowing with milk and honey. To enter the Promised Land was a bold move for the children of Israel, as God instructed them to kill all the people inhabiting Canaan, the Promised Land, including the women and children (Joshua 9:24).

Moses sent twelve scouts to the Promised Land. Their mission was to investigate and determine if the giants inhabiting the land could be conquered. There was one scout representing each of the twelve tribes of Israel. The ten scouts with the majority reported the land was flowing with milk and honey but the land was inhabited by giants. The minority report given by Joshua and Caleb confirmed the majority report with one exception. They reported that the giants inhabiting the land could be conquered because the Lord was on their side. Despite having heard Joshua and Caleb's report, the children of Israel were still too afraid of the giants and refused to enter the land (Numbers 14:1-4).

For their disobedience, God severely punished the children of Israel. For their punishment, they would die in the wilderness. However, there was one exception — Joshua, Caleb and the children of Israel's descendants 19 years and younger would enter the Land 40 years later (Numbers 14:20-38).

My analysis of Dr. King's speech and my biblical readings were constantly on my mind. A few weeks after my meeting with the local pastor, for no apparent reason, I awoke with the year 1964 on my mind. The digital clock on my nightstand registered 4:30 a.m. Since sleep eluded me, I decided to get up and start my 5 a.m. morning walk earlier than usual. Less than 25 yards into my walk, I again became preoccupied with 1964. Out of frustration, I blurted out loud, "Speak Lord, your child is listening."

The year 2004 then flashed into my thoughts. Immediately it dawned on me that the difference between 1964, the year Congress passed the Civil Rights Act, and 2004 is 40 years. My fear of the 40-year revelation and not knowing its meaning caused anxiety and I quickened my pace. I hurried home and waited somewhat impatiently until half past six to pick up my telephone. Although it was an early hour, I called the prominent pastor of yet another large black congregation. I apologized for the early hour and explained my urgency by sharing with him my experience. I told him, "I do not know what is going on in my life." During our conversation, I was overcome with emotion. He reminded me that we were in the Lenten period and suggested that I go by the church to pick up a complimentary book, "Events of the Original Lenten Season,"[13] which detailed the season of Lent. His parting counsel was, "Stay in prayer and the Lord will reveal what he has in store for you."

Later that day, I went by the church, picked up the book and began reading it that night. The book depicted Jesus' last 40 days before his crucifixion as chronicled in the gospels of Matthew, Mark, Luke and John. To be honest, while I had read verses from each Gospel, never before had I read an entire Gospel in one session. In my mind, this provided no comfort because although I did not know what I was searching for, I was certain this wasn't it. More than three years later, while taking my morning walk in August 2006, I realized how wrong I had been. At that time, I understood that this spiritual journey concerned black people's missing history before, during and after Jesus' lifetime. I later learned that this missing history may contribute to the inability of black people to unify and confront the economic challenges endangering the community.

I stayed in prayer and returned to my readings of the first five books of the Bible. The continuous reading strengthened my belief about the parallel. The more I went back and forth reading the Bible and Dr. King's speech, the more convinced I became there was a parallel between the progress of the Civil Rights Movement and the progress of the children of Israel leaving Egypt and camping at Mount Sinai.

A friend loaned me Taylor Branch's CD of "*At Canaan's Edge.*"[14] It was so informative that I purchased the book. Branch reports that Civil Rights activists, Andrew Young and James Bevel, in action reminiscent of Joshua and Caleb scouting the Promised Land, scouted Lowndes County, Alabama to gauge interest for a

Selma to Montgomery March. The march would proceed to the state capital to appeal for black people's right to vote.

My journey had begun to reveal a parallel between black people who came to America as slaves and their descendants and the children of Israel who were held captive in Egypt. It appears that both groups endured extremely long periods of captivity. I knew I was going in the right direction when I read that Dr. King made reference to the parallel in his book, *Where Do We Go From Here: Chaos or Community?*, as it appears in *A Testament of Hope – The Essential Writings and Speeches of Martin Luther King, Jr.*[15] He wrote: "The Bible tells the thrilling story of how Moses stood in Pharaoh's court centuries ago and cried, 'Let my people go.' This was an opening chapter in a continuing story. The present struggle in the United States is a later chapter in the same story. Something within has reminded the Negro of his birthright of freedom, and something without has reminded him that it can be gained." This may be a later chapter in the same story indeed but the story appears to continue developing.

Even though Dr. King wrote there was a parallel between the children's escape from Egypt and the Civil Rights Movement in his book, I knew that I needed strong evidence to convince today's black people. Like the disciples who doubted that Jesus had risen and needed more proof by examining the wounds, I knew I had to prove this parallel with actual biblical text, chapter and verse.

First, I had to establish for myself that God spoke directly to Dr. King — as he did to Moses — who was afraid to lead the children of Israel. It is noted that God spoke to Moses in the book of Exodus, 3:10-12, "Now go, for I am sending you to Pharaoh. You will lead my people, the Israelites, out of Egypt."

"But who am I to appear before Pharaoh?" Moses asked God. "How can you expect me to lead the Israelites out of Egypt?" Then God told him, "I will be with you."

In his book, *Bearing The Cross,* David J. Garrow, notes that in 1955 Dr. King was elected by blacks in Montgomery, Alabama, to lead the Montgomery Bus Boycott. Dr. King tells how he was overcome with fear after receiving death threats and was thinking of a way to back out of his leadership position without looking like a coward. This is reminiscent of Moses being afraid to lead the children of Israel. Dr. King recalled while at home on a Friday night in January 1955, "after his brief sojourn at the Montgomery County jail," his confidence was at an all-time low. As he was preparing for bed, he received a death threat by telephone. He hung up the phone and went to bed but could not sleep. He got out of bed, went to the kitchen, prepared a cup of coffee and reflected on how God had promised never to leave him alone. Dr. King said:

> *"I prayed a prayer, and I prayed out loud that night. I said, 'Lord, I'm down here trying to do what's right. I think I'm right. I think the cause that we represent is right. But Lord, I must confess that I'm weak now. I'm faltering. I'm losing my courage. And I can't let the people see me like this because if they see me weak and losing my courage, they will begin to get weak.'*

*Then it happened: And it seemed at that mo-
ment that I could hear an inner voice saying to
me, 'Martin Luther, stand up for righteousness.
Stand up for justice. Stand up for truth. And lo
I will be with you, even until the end of the world.'
... I heard the voice of Jesus saying still to fight
on. He promised never to leave me, never to
leave me alone. No never alone. No never alone.
He promised never to leave me, never to leave
me alone."*

The parallel continues with the comparison of the text of
Dr. King's "Promised Land" speech to biblical accounts of Moses'
spoken word. Early in the speech, Dr. King talks about black
people staying unified. He mentions how the Pharaoh prolonged
the period of slavery by keeping the slaves fighting among themselves. When the slaves came together, it was the beginning of
their release from slavery. The book of Exodus, 5:6-23, talks
about the Pharaoh taking away straw (and essential ingredient of
brick making) to make the captives' task of brick-making harder
and how this hardship caused them to complain to Moses, thus
prolonging the period of slavery.

Dr. King was deeply concerned about the non-violent Civil
Rights Movement losing unity and momentum and being upstaged
by the violent Black Power movement advocated by Floyd
McKissick, national director of the Congress of Racial Equality
(CORE) and Stokely Carmichael, who was with the Student Non-
violent Coordinating Committee (SNCC). The Black Power move-

ment was gaining momentum a year after the passage of the Voting Rights Act of 1965 and gained a new momentum in Greenwood, Mississippi.

In June 1965, James Meredith was shot while attempting the first stage of his Freedom March through Mississippi. In his book, At Canaan's Edge, Taylor Branch recounts the day after Meredith's shooting, Dr. King, McKissick and Carmichael met with Meredith and told him his march should be continued to show the world that blacks would not be intimidated by white terrorists. The day after visiting Meredith in the hospital, Dr. King, McKissick and Carmichael started the second stage of Meredith's march through Mississippi.

While marching, it became apparent to Dr. King that McKissick, Carmichael and others were becoming disenchanted with the non-violence platform of the Civil Rights Movement. Several of the marchers expressed frustration and anger with the violence carried out against them by white racists and wanted to know why the march needed the participation of white supporters. There were comments about changing the words to the song, "We Shall Overcome" to "We Shall Overrun." This notion disturbed Dr. King immensely. His response to the supporters of violence was, "The formidable foe we now faced demanded more unity than ever before and that I would stretch every point to maintain this unity, but that I could not in good conscience agree to continue my personal involvement and that of SCLC [Southern Christian Leadership Conference] in the march if it were not publicly affirmed that it was based on non-violence and the participation of both black and white."

Much to Dr. King's dismay, a few days later at an evening rally in Greenwood, Stokely Carmichael stirred the crowd by shouting, "What we need is black power." While the term "Black Power," had been used before, the rally in Greenwood gave the slogan life.

The Bible's book of Exodus notes that the children of Israel's 400-year ordeal of captivity in Egypt came to an end through the diligence of a leader, Moses — and through God performing mighty miracles. In his speech, "I Have a Dream" delivered on the steps of the Lincoln Memorial, Dr. King referenced the fact that 100 years earlier, Abraham Lincoln signed the Emancipation Proclamation that freed the slaves. Although the law was passed in 1863 to free the slaves, blacks were still not free 100 years later. When Congress voted into law the Civil Rights Act of 1964, for the first time, black people had formally recognized and enforced civil rights in the United States of America.

When the Civil Rights Act was passed, it was a replay of the same old story. Just like the children of Israel escaped Egypt after 400 years of captivity and realized that they were not free until they entered the Promised Land, so too, have black people realized they have yet to enter the Promised Land in the U.S.A. In other words, blacks have not acquired the ability or been provided the opportunity to accumulate wealth like other ethnic groups.

The opportunity to accumulate wealth was delayed by slavery and the era of Jim Crow and the commonly held notion that once freed of their shackles, African-Americans would succeed because the playing field was level. Put another way, even if the field is level, the team with the least resources is more likely than not to lose. In those odd situations where the underdog wins we call that team the "miracle" or "Cinderella team." But, African-Americans have not seen glass slippers. They have only seen *glass ceilings*.

Even though the Civil Rights Act was passed in 1964 allowing a black person the right to enter any restaurant establishment, the Act meant nothing when the individual was without money to pay the tab at the end of the meal. And although the Fair Housing Act, which passed in 1965, allows a black person the right to live in any neighborhood, the Act means nothing without money to make the monthly mortgage payment. The legislation passed by Congress is a worthless promissory note if you have no money in the bank. Many blacks realize that not gaining a share of the nation's wealth prolongs the dire economic conditions and stagnant poverty still thriving in much of the black community. In point of fact, this was the same condition that blacks found themselves in throughout the South after the Emancipation Proclamation in 1863 and the end of the Reconstruction Era in 1877.

I draw a parallel between the slavery of Moses' time and the social and economic bondage of Dr. King's time. One has to look at what happened to the Civil Rights Movement after Dr. King's death. What arose in the wake of his death were serious disagreements among blacks in terms of resolving economic troubles, along with social, political and moral challenges.

I assert that an important cause of this confusion is the lack of a clear sense of identity. These same squabbles were engaged in by the children of Israel after their escape from bondage in Egypt. Much to Moses' horror, many of the Israelites argued the case to go back into their earlier bondage.

The lack of a true sense of identity for African-Americans reflects, in large measure the reality that, unlike Alex Haley in his seminal work, *Roots*, most black Americans cannot trace their lineage with significant accuracy back to Africa. We are left with our faith, curiosity and immediate history. My desire is that we find our way together, for as I found, blacks have a real tangible and historical identity.

When I began my journey, the parallels between African-Americans and the Israelites were not evident to me. I didn't know at the time that my journey would become spiritual. The combination of learning about Dr. King's life and the biblical readings of Moses allowed me to see the parallel clearly. I began to understand that something monumental was happening in my life.

Chapter 3 – In Whose Image?

"My momma borned (sic) me in a ghetto! There was no mattress for my head. But, No! She couldn't call me 'Jesus' "I wasn't white enough, she said."

The lyrics to "Kung Fu" by Rhythm and Blues singing legend Curtis Mayfield were etched in my memory over thirty years ago. Radical, even by today's standards, they raise a question many blacks have privately pondered. "What *did* Jesus look like?" In fact, Christ was a Jew, a Semite, and at a minimum probably looked most like the darker-skinned Arabs of today.

While I still hold with the Baptist teachings of my childhood, I now attend the Catholic Church. These lyrics came to mind during Mass a couple of years after my speech to the giants. The priest's homily was about Sister Maria Faustina and her image of Jesus Christ. We have all seen the image of Jesus that is displayed in many Catholic Churches. As I listened to the story, there was something about it and the image of Jesus that seemed not quite right. According to the Catholic Church, this image was conceived on February 22, 1931, by Sister Faustina who was born Helen Kowalska. Her name was changed to Sister Faustina when she became a nun.

On February 22, 1931, in her convent cell, Sister Faustina claimed Jesus appeared and instructed her to paint an image of Him, "…according to the pattern you see with the inscription: Jesus,

I trust in You!" According to her diary, the Lord showed her several visions and taught her different prayers. Many years later on April 30, 2000, Pope John Paul II canonized her as Saint Maria Faustina Kowalska. *See the color plate insert* for a representation of the vision Sister Faustina related.

Helen Kowalska was born in Glogowiec, Poland on August 25, 1905. Around the age of 20, she entered the "convent of the Congregation of Sisters of Our Lady of Mercy on Zytnia Street in Warsaw." She lived there from August 1, 1925 to her death on October 5, 1938. In the preface of her diary, which was written by Andrew M. Deskur, Titular Archbishop of Tene states: "The reader, after just a superficial skimming of the 'Diary,' may be struck by the simplicity of the language and even by the spelling and stylistic errors, but he should not forget that the author of the Diary had but a limited elementary education."

In Sister Faustina's memoirs, Diary of Saint Maria Faustina Kowalska, — Divine Mercy in My Soul, in October 1937, one year before her death, she writes; "My Jesus, You know that from my earliest years I have wanted to become a great saint; that is to say, I have wanted to love You with a love so great that there would be no soul who has hitherto love You so. At first these desires of mine were kept secret, **(23)** and only Jesus knew of them. But today I cannot contain them within my heart; I would like to cry out to the whole world, 'Love God, because he is good and great is His mercy!'"

It appears, from the aforementioned writings in Sister Faustina's diary that she held very high spiritual aspirations. While we cannot be certain of her innermost thoughts, it is likely that her vision of Jesus was influenced by what most Europeans already believed he looked like. After all, she was a white European who was born, raised and died in Poland?

****

While many blacks have always been devout Christians, some still respect alternative biblical interpretations put forth by black leaders such as Marcus Garvey and Elijah Muhammad. Such leaders have advanced arguments asserting that the true images of God and Jesus Christ are not the European-looking images to which most Christians are exposed. Most cultures—except African-Americans in general— portray Christ as looking like them!

The alternative theory is that the Original Man created by God was in fact, black. For years when discussing this subject with black friends, they always mentioned Jesus' description as noted in the books of Revelation and Daniel. Sister Faustina's image of a fair-skinned man with flowing blond hair certainly did not match the biblical description of Jesus! After listening to the priest's message, I decided to conduct personal research.

One of my pastor friends provided desperately needed counsel, assisted with valuable research and loaned me his copy of a book by John L. Johnson, *The Black Biblical Heritage*.[16] Johnson's book chronicles biblical characters from a black perspective. I also viewed a televised documentary titled, *"The Real Eve,"*[17] which was produced in 2002 and narrated by actor Danny Glover. It examined the question of whether Eve, the first woman, originated in Ethiopia. For me, it has become exceedingly difficult to ignore those who question the traditional descriptions of the most prominent individuals in the Bible.

The prophet Daniel recorded his vision of Jesus over 500 years before Jesus' birth. In the *Holy Bible – King James Version - Family Reference Edition,*[18] the verses read:

> *"Then I lifted up mine eyes, and looked, and behold a certain man clothed in linen, whose loins were girded with fine gold of U'-phaz: His body also was like the beryl, and his face as the appearance of lightning, and his eyes as lamps of fire, and **his arms and his feet like in color to polished brass**, and the voice of his words like the voice of a multitude." (Daniel 10:5-6).*

According to the *Life Application Study Bible* (LASB),[19] "The book of Revelation was written, "to reveal the full identity of Christ and to give warning and hope to believers. The apostle John [who wrote the book of Revelation] had been an eyewitness of the incarnate Christ, had a vision of the glorified Christ." As recorded in Revelation 1:14-15 in the Holy Bible Family Reference Edition:

> *"**His head and his hairs were white like wool, as white as snow;** and his eyes were as a flame of fire; And **his feet like unto fine brass, as if they burned in a furnace;** and his voice as the sound of many waters."*

If you drew or painted a picture of Jesus Christ based on the biblical description of his skin color as noted by Daniel and the biblical description of his hair and skin color as noted by the apostle John, would it look like Sister Faustina's vision? Where are the hairs white like wool and the complexion of brass as if burned in a furnace? *See the color plate insert.*

We all know that someone with even a minimal elementary education can identify the color white. When I did my own unscientific survey about Sister Faustina's painting of Jesus, the description of his hair that I heard most often was that the color was sandy, reddish brown or sandy blond. As nobody ever mentioned seeing white hair, I concluded it either was not in the painting or that it was not obvious to the casual observer.

While looking at the color of the sheep's fleece or woolly coat, notice the texture. Could apostle John have also been trying to describe the texture of Jesus' hair as looking like wool? It appears that the texture is strikingly like that of an Ethiopian or a person of direct African ancestry. *See the color plate insert.*

Similarly, when we consider the biblical description of Jesus' skin color, he is described as having "feet unto fine brass, as if they burned in a furnace." The key word, "burned," is defined as "to become charred or overcooked." When something or someone looks "charred," it or they are almost black. This leads me to think "burned in a furnace" refers to a person with a dark complexion.

As written in Daniel 10:5-6, Jesus had a "voice of a multitude." Or, as written in Revelation 1:14-15, Jesus had a "voice as the sound of many waters." If someone asked me to describe

Jesus, based on the biblical descriptions in Daniel and Revelation, I would say he had a bass baritone voice and physique similar to that of the late actor Paul Robeson.

The apostle John personally knew Jesus and could give a vivid description of him. So, why is it that the commonly accepted images of Jesus are so far removed from John's personal description? Surely, John knew the difference between white and blond hair and light and dark skin. Maybe this is why John chose to liken Jesus' hair to white like a sheep's wool — to emphasize the color and texture of Christ's hair. Maybe this is why John chose to liken Jesus' skin to burned brass — to emphasize that Christ's skin color was undeniably dark.

****

We have been told human beings are created in God's image — a point clearly stated in the Bible. Some may argue that the only thing that matters is our behavior and how well we adhere to the will of God and the teachings of Jesus Christ. They may regard this book's discussion about the racial background and physical appearance of Adam and Eve and their descendants as irrelevant.

Being born "colored" in the segregated South, with God-fearing parents and relatives, many of my early beliefs were shaped by what I witnessed as a boy. I saw hardship, overt racism, hatred, resentment, fear and a people whose known family history starts as chattel traded on an auction block.

When one considers the age-old persecution of darker-

complexioned races for supposedly being inferior and destructive, it does indeed matter to discern and understand the coura-
geous leadership and sacrifices made throughout biblical times by
men and women of sub-Saharan African ancestry.

By the time I had drawn my own conclusions about Sister
Faustina's vision, I was eager to discuss what I had found in the
Bible. A cousin, Rhonda Brown, suggested focusing on the story
of Noah and his three sons. After reading the story, I became
interested in Noah's son Ham when the footnote mentioned Genesis 9:25 being used to support racial prejudice and slavery. See
the LASB, page 20.

Whenever I hear or read the words, "racial prejudice" and
"slavery," I automatically think it's about black people. There
was more curiosity when I read the biblical accounts of Ham's
grandson, Nimrod, the great-grandson of Noah. Not being a
reader of the Bible, and hearing the name Nimrod mentioned only
in a negative way, I thought Nimrod was a bad character.

The word "nimrod" which was originally used to mean "a
mighty hunter" has come to mean idiot or jerk. A derivation of
"nimrod" is "nincompoop" — an individual who is stupid or foolish. And another derivation, "ninny" refers to a fool or someone
who's slow-witted or a blockhead.

When I read the biblical accounts of Nimrod, I was surprised to read that he was "a heroic warrior, a mighty hunter in the
Lord's sight" and a builder of empires (Genesis 10:8-12). On
page 44 in the Dictionary of the Holy Bible Family Reference Edition, Nimrod was written about as being a legend. His definition
reads; "a legendary hero of the Mesopotamian region. The leg-

ends may have grown around the Babylonian war god Ninurta, or a historical figure, the Assyrian king Tukulti-Ninurta (1246-1206 B.C.), the first Assyrian to rule over all Babylonia. Nimrod son of Cush has the legendary greatness." It appears that historians, both secular and faith-based, have gone out of their way to belittle or erase Nimrod's place in history.

Maybe we should ask ourselves, how a man of such stature could have his importance in history rewritten to the point where his name is associated with legends and fiction and with something ridiculous or foolish? The name Nimrod today implies dullard, which sits in complete opposition to the word of God as written in the book of Genesis 10:8-12.

Reading the fabricated description of Nimrod caused me to reflect on the name of his grandfather, Ham. There are negative images associated with his name as well. Most of us have heard of someone being referred to as a "ham," which has been defined as an actor who overdoes it during a performance or "ham-handed," which means, clumsy or inept.

I knew I was on to something, but I needed more proof. Like Jesus' disciple, Thomas, I needed to see and touch the wounds in order to believe (John 20:25). My Bible would be continuously read to seek answers. If the "Original Man" legend was true, there had to be evidence in the scripture. The first clue came while reading Genesis 2:13 in the Holy Bible Family Reference Edition. In this chapter and verse, the word "Ethiopia" is first mentioned: "And the name of the second river is Gihon: the same is it that compasseth the whole land of Ethiopia." In the LASB, the word "Ethiopia" is translated to read "Cush." As I had been doing my initial study in the LASB, I had not yet come across the word "Ethiopia" found in the KJV 1611 Holy Bible. I did not realize the names "Cush" and "Ethiopia" were synonymous.

Webster's defines "Ethiopia" as "an ancient region in Northeast Africa, bordering on Egypt and the Red Sea." "Ethiope" or "Ethiop" is the Old English version of the word, "Ethiopia." According to the *Oxford English Dictionary* (OED), an Ethiopian is "a person with a black skin, a blackamoor – a Negro or any dark-skinned person." An Ethiopian is also defined by the *Random House College Dictionary* as "a member of any of various supposedly dark-skinned peoples regarded by the ancients as coming from a country lying south of Egypt." The OED[20] has a phrase that appears in Volume V, page 423, which reads; "to wash an Ethiop (white): to attempt the impossible." Also, according to the OED, some anthropologists believe at least "one of the races into which the human species is divided" comes from the Ethiopians. There will be more on the "Ethiopian" association with dark skin in the chapter titled, "Adam's Skin Color."

One could conclude from these findings that changing the name of the country "Ethiopia" in Genesis 2:13 to the name of its inhabitants "Cush" may be perceived as obscuring or attempting to erase black people's role in the Bible. Without wanting to be accusatory, it does appear theologians who translated the Bible have been successful. Most descendants of black people who came to America as slaves cannot trace their roots beyond the boundaries of the U.S.A. I wonder if this knowledge regarding the removal of the word "Ethiopia" could be the reason for today's descendants of black people not knowing or even realizing that they could attempt to trace their ancestral roots beyond the U.S.A. and even as far back as the original descendants of Adam and Eve.

****

These are my final comments on Ethiopia. On Tuesday, June 19, 2007, the Houston Chronicle printed an article titled, Mysterious kingdom of Kush had more than just gold," by John Noble Wilford, New York Times. The article was of interest because it talks about "Kush" (also spelled Cush), the inhabitants of Ethiopia before the birth of Christ, without mentioning the name "Kush" being associated with Ethiopia or Ethiopians.

The article mentions how archaeologist found evidence of a complex society in Africa. "From deciphered Egyptian documents and modern archaeological research, it is now known that for five centuries in the second millennium B.C., the kingdom of Kush flourished with the political and military prowess to maintain some control over a wide territory in Africa."

Not once in the article was the word black or any association with black people mentioned. Only the word "sub-Saharan" provides a hint of blackness. From reading this article, it appears that in the year 2007, the obscuration of black people's history for whatever reason continues.

The discovery of "Ethiopia" had a maddening head-spinning impact and I would later make a new friend from the 14th Century — Sir John Mandeville.

Chapter 4 – Moment of Discovery

I started my Labor Day 2006 morning walk under a cloudy, overcast sky that literally turned sunny after I received a long-awaited revelation. With this revelation, I felt for the first time that I was able to understand and interpret several key biblical verses. The words of my former high school typing teacher reverberated, "Willie, would you recognize it [what you are seeking], if the Lord showed it to you?" My reply at the time was, I didn't know.

Athletes are famously superstitious and always on the lookout for signs. An inner voice told me to look for the month, day and year that totaled 19, a number that was to be significant. Number 19 is the number I wore on my college and professional football jerseys, and is directly associated with my fame and public recognition. Number 19 also is the number on the Willie Alexander-Houston Oilers doll my son would call for each night before my wife or I tucked him into bed. When the revelation awakened me that Labor Day morning, it was during my walk that I recognized the sign. Many mornings I had awakened with ideas for the manuscript. This morning was different. When the numbers in the date 09-04-06 added up to 19, there was no doubt I recognized what the Lord was showing me.

Not only did I recognize the revelation; it was confirmed when I realized it came on a predicted date. A month earlier back in August 2006, I telephoned a friend and thanked him for loaning his Dr. Martin Luther King CDs several years earlier in August 2003. At that time, the King CDs inspired me to purchase the book, *A Testament of Hope: Essential Writings of Dr. Martin Luther King.* Reading the books within the book was inspirational during the early stages of this journey. One of the books inside the *Essential Writings* was, *Where Do We Go from Here: Chaos or Community?*

Reading this book provided significant information. For an unknown reason, which later became clear, I wrote my friend's name and the date, Thursday, 8/7/03, on the book's first page. Three years later in the same month and on the same day I called and thanked him for sharing the CDs three years earlier.

To fully comprehend the revelation, the reader must have a general understanding of how the Bible was written. The biblical stories were recounted as parables. A parable is defined by Webster's Dictionary as a short story of symbolic meaning designed to convey a truth or moral lesson and a statement that conveys a meaning indirectly by the use of comparison, analogy, or the like.

In the Bible, the metaphor is used as a figure of speech applied to suggest a resemblance — as in "A mighty fortress is our God." If the prophet Moses read a modern-day manuscript during ancient times, he would have assumed it was written metaphorically. During Moses' time, most people could not read or write. It's logical that Moses used images to symbolize the meaning of words in the same way that we consult the dictionary to define words. In Moses' time, any writer would have to use descriptive images with characteristics that the listener would recognize.

Today, when someone is called a "dog," we know the person is not literally a "dog" as in being a domesticated canine, but figuratively, "an ugly, boring or crude person." When a person says someone is "cool," we know the person is not literally "cool" as being "neither warm nor cold" but figuratively "cool," exhibiting "calmness; composure; poise."

With this understanding of the comparison of ancient and modern writing styles, biblical words take on different meanings. I now better understand what is meant when it is said the Bible is written metaphorically; "the application of a word or phrase to an object or concept it does not literally denote, in order to suggest comparison with another object or concept," as in "... upon this rock I will build my church..." (Matthew 16:18).

The *King James Version Hebrew-Greek Key Word Study Bible,*[21] a biblical dictionary, is silent on the definition of all words in Genesis 2:10: "And a river went out of Eden to water the garden; and from thence it was parted, and became into four heads." A month earlier, I had sat in my attorney's office and discussed this very verse. For more than a month, the Genesis 2:10 mystery had teased and tantalized. When I awakened on September 4, an inner voice said, return to the dictionary and take another look at the definition of the word, "river." By looking at that definition one more time, I discovered, I had inadvertently overlooked a second meaning of "river" as noted in all of the dictionaries.

The unabridged dictionary at my home, revealed a second definition of "river" ("rive" + "er," pronounced "r(y)ver" – "a person who r(y)ves"). I am defining both root words of the word "river" to illustrate their importance in how "river" is used in the cited biblical verse.

The word pronounced "r(y)ver" originated around the years 1475-85. This time period is 126 years before the writing of the original King James Version of the Holy Bible, written in 1611. What seemed a mystery was now becoming clearer. The definition of "r(y)ve," is "to tear or rend," or "to harrow or distress (the heart) with painful feelings." The definition of the suffix, "er" represents pause or hesitation.

When combining the words, "r(y)ve" and "er," I can see a new meaning of the word "river" in the context of Genesis 2:10. A month earlier, I thought the "river" represented Adam and Eve. However, there were no reference points to confirm what I thought in my biblical resources. Therefore, I consulted the dictionary for the definition of other key words just as I had done for "river."

The definition of "went" in its root word, "go," is "to leave a place." The LASB substitutes the word "went" with "flow." Two definitions of "flow" mean "to menstruate or to come or go as in a stream; A constant stream of humanity flowed by." A non medical use of the word "water," to this day, is "breaking water," which is used to describe the moment a woman is about to go into labor. I believe the reference to "water" in this context suggests Eve — as a "r(y)ver" — is pregnant.

The next key word is "parted," which is defined as "heraldry" — "of tracing and recording genealogies." The last key word is "head." The LASB translates "head" to "branch," which provides a clearer meaning. The word "branch" is defined as "a line of family descent stemming from a particular ancestor, as distinguished from some other line or lines from the same stock; a division of a family."

When I look at the definition of all the words in question — "r(y)ver," "went," "water," "parted," and "branch" — the verse begins to reveal a developing story. At this point, I believe the "river" (ryver) symbolizes Adam and Eve. It appears Adam and Eve left the Garden of Eden and Eve was pregnant. From her child-birth, descendants would eventually overspread the earth. As the well-known biblical story goes, Adam and Eve disobeyed God by eating the forbidden fruit after Eve was tricked by the "serpent." This disobedience resulted in them being banished from the Garden of Eden.

With this newly-found "defined word approach," applied to Genesis 2:10, I now asked myself, did Adam and Eve actually eat fruit or is the "fruit" a metaphor? If not an apple, what was the forbidden fruit? Who was the "serpent?" Did Eve actually talk to a snake? Why were Adam and Eve banished from the Garden of Eden and what did "banishment" mean? In adopting this new approach, I would apply it later to other biblical verses.

****

Wednesday, September 20, 2006 was a typical day, or so I thought. The business day started with a 10 a.m. client presentation. Afterward, I attended a luncheon hosted by a friend in honor of his former law partner. The gathering was a distinguished group comprised of lawyers and various other professionals. After lunch, I headed to downtown Houston to attend a regularly scheduled law school board of trustees meeting.

The board meeting proceeded as usual, with one exception. An announcement was made about a complimentary giveaway of a book written by one of the law school's professors, Mark E. Steiner. I briefly examined the book, *An Honest Calling,—The Law Practice of Abraham Lincoln,* and decided to give the professor a call in the near future. Since I was writing a book and his was recently published, I thought he could provide helpful advice about how to get my own book published. The board meeting adjourned and an announcement was made regarding a faculty reception following the meeting. On the way out of the boardroom, I paused at the reception to say hello to several of the faculty members before heading back to my office.

To my surprise, out of the crowd stepped Professor Steiner, whose book I was holding. I remember saying; "It is so good to see you as one item on my agenda is to give you a call." We chatted, and before long, I was briefing him on the manuscript for Entering the Promised Land. I told him one of my challenges was defining words not found in the King James Version Hebrew-Greek Key Word Study Bible and Webster's Unabridged Dictionary. He suggested I look in The Oxford English Dictionary and also said the dictionaries are in the law school library. After our chat, I headed straight for the library.

As I approached the library, memories of my fifth grade homeroom teacher resonated. Even today, I can vividly remember her teaching us the meaning of the word, "library." I can still hear her saying, "The library is a storehouse of information." She went on to add, "Being smart is not walking around with a lot of information in your head. Being smart is knowing where to find the information you are seeking."

On this day at the law school, I walked into a storehouse of information. I found the dictionaries and proceeded to look up the word "east." Reading one of the many definitions of the word "east," led me to the discovery of the word "Maundev." The law school librarian informed me that "Maundev" was the abbreviation for the author, Sir John Mandeville. This knowledge led me to the book, The Travels of Sir John Mandeville. This information would prove to be a monumental breakthrough in my research.

The word "east" was of interest because it appears for the first time in the Bible's book of Genesis 2:8 and 2:14. Genesis 2:8 reads – "Then the Lord God planted a garden in Eden, in the east, and there he placed the man he had created." According to this verse, Adam was not created in the Garden of Eden and came from elsewhere. The burning question is where?

Chapter 5 – Defined Word Approach

To answer the burning question of where Adam was created, I remembered a minister's parting instructions: "Willie, start your biblical readings in the book of Genesis, Chapter 37. From there, proceed reading the book of Exodus and the other books in the Pentateuch." As I followed the minister's instructions, I wasn't certain about what I was trying to find.

Something compelled me to go back and start at the beginning of the Bible. I read Chapter One in Genesis, The Creation, then Chapter Two, the story of Adam and Eve. I became fascinated with the story of Adam and figuratively set up camp. After continuous reading, the story made no sense. Finally, on Labor Day 2006 the revelation came that unlocked the scripture's interpretation with a discovery, I later named the "defined word approach." This approach allowed me to return to the chapter, "In Whose Image?" to confirm my understanding of previously interpreted scripture.

The reader may ask, what is this new-found "defined word approach?" The approach assists with the interpretation of the translated 1611 Holy Bible. The key word I am emphasizing is "translated," which means put into the words of a different language. There is a warning at the end of the book of Revelation regarding changing any of the original biblical text. This warning in the book of Revelation 22:18-19, as found in the KJV, reads:

"For I testify unto every man that heareth the words of the prophecy of this book, If any man shall add unto these things, God shall add unto him the plagues that are written in this book: And if any man shall take away from the words of the book of this prophecy, God shall take away his part out of the book of life, and out of the holy city, and from the things which are written in this book."

According to the LASB, a translation of the 1611 Holy Bible, there are two general theories — or methods — of Bible translation. The LASB denotes the first theory as "formal equivalence." According to this theory, the translator attempts to convert each word of the original language [Hebrew, Aramaic or Greek] into the equivalent of the receiving language [English] and seeks to preserve the original word order and sentence structure as much as possible.

The second theory is called "dynamic equivalence or functional equivalence." The goal of this translation theory is to produce in the receiving language the closest natural equivalent of the message expressed by the original language text, both in meaning and in style. Such a translation attempts to have the same impact on modern readers as the original had on its audience.

A dynamic equivalence translation can also be called a thought-for-thought translation, as contrasted with a formal equivalence — or word-for-word translation.

In making a thought-for-thought translation, the translators must do their best to enter into the thought pattern of the ancient authors and to present the same ideas, connotations, and effects in the receiving language.

For purposes of this manuscript, I will proceed with the understanding that the thought-for-thought translations by other biblical scholars are accurate. I am well aware that this assumption leaves my work subject to some criticism, but I am persuaded that it does not materially alter the efficacy of my findings.

In my interpretations, I will use a word-for-word translation methodology. Specifically, this methodology allows the meaning of the translated word(s) to create the story.

First, I define the key word(s) in a Bible verse. Second, I define each key word within the definition of a key word or words. Third, when necessary, I use The OED's quotations it borrows from other literature to demonstrate the meaning of various words. This approach details the meaning of each word to help communicate and clarify metaphorical meanings in biblical stories.

Please note the etymology of most key words in this book predate the 1611 Holy Bible and were defined first, in most cases, by the OED. This particular dictionary is noted for its use of quotations and extensive definitions of words as written in the English language as it was spoken in the Middle Ages — long before the publication of the King James Version of the Bible in 1611. *Random House Webster's Unabridged Dictionary*[22] and *Random House College Dictionary*[23] were also resource tools.

The dictionary defines etymology as the study of historical linguistic change, especially as applied to individual words. It also provides an account of the history of a particular word and the derivation of a word. Armed with this new way of understanding words, I returned to an earlier written chapter, "In Whose Image?", and applied the "approach" to the words "brass and burned," found in Revelation 1:14-15. The application of the "approach" confirmed that Jesus' skin color was black. As the saying goes in auto racing, "Gentlemen start your engines."

Chapter 6 – The Truth Shall Rise

My research for this book cites essays attributed to a 14th century English author who used the pen name of Sir John Mandeville. An article in The New Encyclopaedia Britannica[24] discredits the likelihood of Mandeville being the person who actually traveled and recorded what he saw. The article states that the Mandeville essays are "selections from the narratives of genuine travelers, embellished with Mandeville's additions and described as his own adventures. It is not certain whether the book's true author ever traveled at all, since he selected his materials almost entirely from the encyclopaedias and travel books available to him, including those by the Catholic missionaries William of Boldensele and Friar Odoric of Pordenone."

The Mandeville essays detail how the author — or the explorers quoted in the essays — located an important travel route in the Holy Land and the surrounding region. What is of specific interest in this book is the author of the Mandeville essays recounts almost word-for-word, one of the most well-known stories of the Bible.

The Travels of Sir John Mandeville recounts the story of how Lot's two daughters got him drunk in order to preserve the family name by having their father unknowingly impregnate them.[25] It is crucial to note the Mandeville book was written more than two and one-half centuries before the publication of the King

James Version of the Holy Bible in 1611.

Apparently, the author had access to an original Hebrew or Greek version of the Bible — meaning the author actually traveled in the Holy Land or cites the work of someone who did. The following is an excerpt in its original Middle English form from the story of Lot as found on page 68 in Chapter 12 of the Mandeville book:

> *"In that city Lot dwelt a little while; and there was he made drunk of his daughters, and lay with them, and engendered of them Moab and Ammon."*

This passage, translated into Modern English, reads:

> *"In that city Lot lived for a short time; and there he was made drunk by his daughters, and [while drunk] he had sexual intercourse with them, and fathered on them Moab and Ammon."*

A fuller version of the biblical story can be found in Genesis 19:30-38 (as it appears in the LASB):

Afterward Lot left Zoar because he was afraid of the people there, and he went to live in a cave in the mountains with his two daughters. One day the older daughter said to her sister, *"There isn't a man anywhere in this entire area for us to marry; And our father will soon be too old to have children. Come, let's get him drunk with wine, and then we will sleep with him. That way we will preserve our family line through our father."*

Above is a replica of the traditional image used to depict Jesus Christ in the Catholic Church.

In the photographs above, note the similarity between the color and texture of my father's hair and the wool of the sheep. I've placed these photos next to each other to illustrate what the apostle John may have been trying to describe when he said Jesus Christ's hair was white like wool and his skin color like brass, as if burned in a furnace.

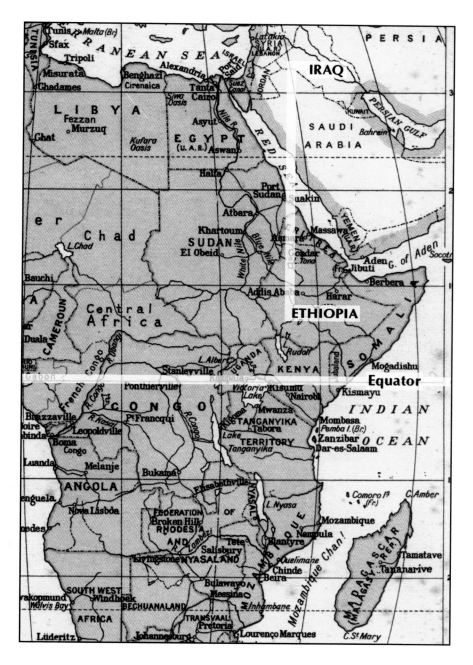

The map above indicates that if someone traveled north from Ethiopia to a point on the horizon and took a 90-degree turn, the traveler would eventually reach Iraq, which many historians cite as the actual location of the Garden of Eden.

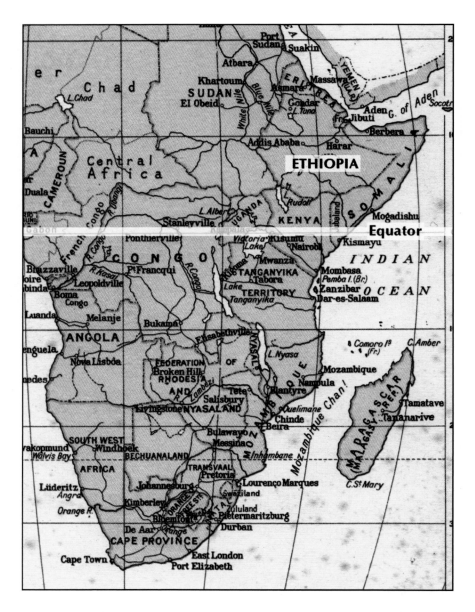

The map above shows the proximity between Ethiopia and the location of the equator. As noted in this book, the daytime temperature in this region averages 122 degrees, while the nighttime temperature averages about 81 degrees. In summary, this region is among the rare places on Earth where — as I contend — it would be understandable for primitive inhabitants such as Adam and Eve to live without clothing.

So that night they got him drunk, and the older daughter went in and slept with her father. He was unaware of her lying down or getting up again.

The next morning the older daughter said to her younger sister, *"I slept with our father last night. Let's get him drunk with wine again tonight, and you go in and sleep with him. That way our family line will be preserved."* That night they got him drunk again, and the younger daughter went in and slept with him. As before, he was unaware of her lying down or getting up again. So both of Lot's daughters became pregnant by their father.

When the older daughter gave birth to a son, she named him Moab. He became the ancestor of the nation now known as the Moabites. When the younger daughter gave birth to a son, she named him Ben-ammi. He became the ancestor of the nation now known as the Ammonites.

Also in Mandeville's book is the quotation, "Ethiope is departed," found in Chapter 17 on page 105. This quotation also appears in The Oxford English Dictionary, Volume V, page 36, which references Sir John Mandeville as "Maundev" in many definitions. The reader should note the OED's Second Edition CD-ROM Version 3.1[26] simply uses "Mandeville" and has discontinued the use of the term "Maundev." When I found the quotation, "Ethiope is departed," in the OED's book version, one of several definitions of the word "east," in Volume 5, page 36, I thought it meant someone was leaving Ethiopia.

I believe the reader will learn the definition of "east" as described in the John Mandeville essays, refers to a route leading from Ethiopia north toward the Mediterranean Sea and then east to a region in present-day Iraq. The region is commonly recognized on most biblical maps as the historic site of the Garden of Eden. This region is first mentioned in the Holy Bible's book of Genesis 2:8: "And the LORD God planted a garden eastward in Eden; and there he put the man whom he had formed." The author of the Mandeville writings asserts he has personally toured northeast Africa and offers a vivid description of the countryside. I will elaborate on the word "east" and the incorporated quotation "Ethiope is departed" in Chapter 8 – The Creation and Migration.

With regard to this book's purpose, the questions about whether the author of the Mandeville essays actually visited and personally documented what is reported about Ethiopia are largely irrelevant. What is relevant is how the Mandeville description of Ethiopia and the route leading from that land to the site of the Garden of Eden is accurate and verifiable. A replica of the Great World Atlas [27] *map is shown in a color plate.*

The aforementioned map indicates the author or authors of the Mandeville essays gave a credible description of Ethiopia and the approximate location of the Garden of Eden in the mid -14th century, more than 250 years before the first publication of the King James Version of the Holy Bible in 1611. Moreover, the Mandeville book corresponds to what is mentioned in the second chapter of Genesis — as will be shown in the chapter titled, "The Creation and Migration."

****

According to a Houston area university medievalist professor's translation, the quotation "Ethiope is departed" reads in its entirety: "Ethiopia is divided in two principal parts and that is the east part and in the meridionelle [southern] part which part meridionelle is called moretane. And the folk of that country are black and now and more black than in the other parts and they are called Moors." The OED references The Travels of Sir John Mandeville in the definitions of "east" and many other words, including: "onyx"; "departed"; "land"; "stranger"; "curse"; "sign"; "mark"; and "compass." The following list shows where these words are located in the OED. The quotations in which the words appear have been translated from Middle to Modern English:

* In Volume 5, page 36 of the OED is the definition of the word "east," as used in a quotation from The Travels of Sir John Mandeville in Chapter 17 on page 105: "Ethiope is departed in two parts principal, and that is in the east part and in the meridional part."

Translation: Ethiopia is divided into two [main] parts; these would be the Eastern section and the Southern section.

* In Volume 10, page 825 of the OED is the definition of the word "onyx" as used in a quotation from The Travels of Sir John Mandeville in Chapter 30, page 182: "One is of onyx, another is of crystal, and another of jasper."

Translation: "One is made of onyx [a semi-precious stone], another one is made of crystal, and another is made of jasper [a semi-precious stone]."

* In Volume 4, page 470 of the OED is the definition of the

word "depart" as used in a quotation from The Travels of Sir John Mandeville in Chapter 6, page 57: "In that ark were the Ten Commandments, and of Aaron's yard, and Moses' yard with the which he made the Red Sea depart."

Translation: In that Ark were contained the Ten Commandments and Aaron's rod, and Moses' rod, with which he parted the Red Sea.

* In Volume 8, page 617 of the OED is the definition of the word "land" as used in a quotation from *The Travels of Sir John Mandeville*, in the Prologue on page 3: "For as much as the land beyond the sea, that is to say the Holy Land, that men call the Land of Promission or of Behest."

Translation: Since it is so that it is the land beyond the sea, that is the Holy Land, which men call the Land of Promise or Promise. ["Behest" is a synonym for promise]

* In Volume 16, page 844 of the OED is the definition of the word "stranger" as used in a quotation from *The Travels of Sir John Mandeville* in Chapter 5, page 20: "And at great feasts, and for strangers, they set forms and tables, as men do in this country, but they had lever sit in the earth."

Translation: And at great feasts, and for foreigners (who visit there) they set out benches and tables, as people do in this country, but they themselves would prefer to sit on the ground.

* In Volume 4, page 154 of the OED is the definition of the word "curse" as used in a quotation from *The Travels of Sir John Mandeville* in Chapter 9, page 48: "For in that book, Mahomet cursed all those that drink wine and all them that sell it."

Translation: For in that book, Mohammed cursed all those

people who drink wine, and also all those who sell wine.

* In Volume 15, page 450 of the OED is the definition of the word "signs" as it appears in a quotation from The Travels of Sir John Mandeville, Chapter 22, page 134: "And therefore they speak not, but they make a manner of hissing as an adder doth, and they make signs one to another as monks do, by the which every of them understandeth other."

Translation: Therefore, they do not speak, but rather they make a type of hissing noise, as an adder [snake] does, and they make gestures to one another as monks do, by which gestures each of them understands one another.

Note: Some medieval monks took vows of silence and communicated by hand gestures. Mandeville is comparing this race of people to monks because they don't speak to communicate; rather, they make a hissing sound or use hand gestures.

* In Volume 9, page 377 of the OED is the definition of the word "mark" as it appears in a quotation from *The Travels of Sir John Mandeville*, Chapter 16, page 97: "In that country of Lybia is the sea more high than the land, and it seemeth that it would cover the earth, and natheles yet it passeth not his marks."

Translation: In that nation of Libya the sea is much higher than the land, and it appears as if it would overwhelm the land, but nevertheless, it does not overflow its boundaries.

* In Volume 3, page 594 of the OED is the definition of the word "compass" as it appears in a quotation from *The Travels of Sir John Mandeville*, Chapter 10, page 50: "And in the midst of the church is a tabernacle, as it were a little house, made with a door, and that tabernacle is made in manner of half a compass."

Translation: "And in the middle of the church is a tabernacle, which resembles a small house, fashioned with a low, small entrance, and that tabernacle is shaped like a semi-circle."

I contend that *The Travels of Sir John Mandeville* is one book that should be translated into Modern English. This translation would make it more readable and more understandable, which I think is necessary because some of its contents precede what is found in the original King James Version of the Bible. Who knows, Mandeville may surprise the reader with other revelations.

****

Dr. Martin Luther King Jr. in his speech, "Facing the Challenge of a New Age," which appears in the book, *A Testament of Hope* said, "There is something in this universe which justifies William Cullen Bryant in saying, 'Truth crushed to earth shall rise again.'" It appears Dr. King was right in suggesting that lies or distortions of truth are never left unchallenged, whether 40 or 650 years later. With my continued study of the Bible, I would later learn that William Cullen Bryant's quote also applies to lies or distortions of the truth dating back to the creation of man.

Chapter 7 - Inspiration in Atlanta

The day was Wednesday, October 25, 2006. I was on the telephone in my car talking to the owner of a publishing company. He also was a pastor and a published author whose book I had read. A local minister had referred me to him.

After going through the normal administrative channels, I was finally engaged in conversation with him and discussing our upcoming meeting in Atlanta. I was so preoccupied that I did not notice that I was driving in a school zone. A police officer soon made me aware of my mistake. I abruptly ended my conversation by telling the publisher that I would call him right back. A traffic ticket later for speeding in the school zone, I resumed the telephone conversation and shared the incident with him. His response was, "Be thankful. The policeman could very well have saved you from running over a child."

We continued our conversation. I shared with him that I had read his book and that it should be required reading for all. We discussed an interpretation of the nursery rhyme, *"Mary Had a Little Lamb."* For readers who are unfamiliar or have forgotten the poem, it reads:

> *Mary had a little lamb,*
> *Its fleece was white as snow;*
> *And everywhere that Mary went,*
> *The lamb was sure to go.*

I told him that when reading the interpretation of the word "fleece," as referring to Jesus' flesh, my thoughts reflected on "fleece," as relating to Jesus' hair as referenced in Revelation 1:14: "His head and his hairs were white like wool, as white as snow." There was silence as if he was considering the interpretation I suggested. When asked the origin of the nursery rhyme he responded that he did not know. I told him that I would do some research and get back to him.

When researching the origin of this nursery rhyme at www.wikipedia.org., I discovered it was first published as a poem by Sarah Hale on May 24, 1830. She was born in New Hampshire as Sarah Sawyer. She wrote the poem after taking her pet lamb to school. Reportedly, her taking the lamb to school caused quite a ruckus and inspired the writing of the poem.

It is not unreasonable to believe that Sarah's poem had biblical undertones. This is because, as noted at www.wikipedia.org, there are two competing theories on the origin of the poem. Either the first four lines of the poem were written by a young man by the name of John Roulstone, who was a nephew and student of the Reverend Lemuel Capen. Or Sarah Hale was responsible for the entire poem (go to www.wikipedia.org for more details).

If Roulstone wrote the lines referring to the color of the lambs fleece it would fit with the revelation of Jesus' hair being described by the apostle John as "white like wool" appears to be described in the nursery rhyme. After reading the apostle John's description of Jesus in Revelation 1:14, I find a striking similarity between apostle John's description of Jesus in the Bible verse and the nursery rhyme. If Sarah wrote the whole poem the biblical connection is not as clear. But, if one notes that the poem is about unwavering but non-romantic or fraternal love, then there is, at least, a reasonable link.

When analyzing the nursery rhyme, I interpret "Mary," as referring to the mother of Jesus Christ and Jesus as the "little lamb." Most Christians are familiar with Jesus being called the "Lamb of God." These words show up in 13 Bible verses, i.e., (John 1:29). It is natural or basic instincts for a child to follow their mother as noted by the words; "And everywhere that Mary went, the lamb was sure to go:" The "fleece," which "was white as snow," represents the hair on Jesus' head. The dictionary defines "fleece," in this context, as the hair on a sheep as "the coat of wool that covers a sheep." It is natural or basic instinct for a child to follow their mother as noted by the words, "and everywhere that Mary went, the lamb was sure to go."

Anyhow, Sarah Hale's nursery rhyme appears to be a dead end. In my opinion, the coincidence that this author used language amazingly similar to biblical scripture is definitely noteworthy.

****

Over the next two weeks, I was pondering Adam and Eve eating the fruit and the serpent's role in their lives. The trip to Atlanta proved to be more than worthwhile.

On November 9, 2006, I met with the publisher. Even though he was in frail health, he spent the entire afternoon listening and counseling my wife and me about my manuscript. He boosted my spirits when he told us that my book, based on research, stood apart from other books on biblical history.*

With his encouraging and inspirational words reverberating in my ears, I returned to Houston with a newly-found inspiration to work on the biblical interpretations. This time I would use a newly-discovered approach to unravel the riddles of the biblical metaphor.

The approach first defines the metaphoric meaning of key words in a Bible verse. If necessary, the approach further defines the meaning of key words within the already defined key word. I was eager to learn if this approach could create a believable story.

****

Thursday morning, January 18, 2007, the alarm clock went off at 4:30 a.m. The bed was as warm and comfortable as the weather outside was cold and miserable. The warmth of the bed prompted me to push the snooze button three times before my feet finally touched the floor at 5 a.m. I turned on the television weather channel to check the outside temperature. It reported a shivering 37 degrees.

Dressed for the weather, I stepped outside, to the cold, damp morning. A light misting rain caught me off guard. A quick trip back inside for my umbrella quickly solved that problem. As usual, I started my walk with a prayer. Shortly into the walk, I reflected upon recent conversations regarding the manuscript.

*Sadly, on December 26, just over a month later, I learned that my friend had passed away three days earlier.

The message from advisors was, "Willie, don't get bogged down giving the reader too much supporting information in the text. It will take away from the main message." It had taken 12 hours of rumination for that to register. Tell the story and let the glossary handle the definitions. The story of "Man in the Garden of Eden" began to unfold.

Arguably, the most well-known Bible story is that of Adam and Eve in the Garden of Eden. The story of Adam in the Garden of Eden is told in second chapter of Genesis before he met Eve. Contrary to popular belief, the Bible does not say Adam, the first man, was created in the Garden of Eden. The Bible does say in Genesis 2:7-8, "And the Lord God formed man of the dust of the ground, and breathed into his nostrils the breath of life; and man became a living soul. And the Lord God planted a garden eastward in Eden; and there he put the man whom he had formed." If Adam was not created in the Garden of Eden, where was he created?

Chapter 8 - The Creation and Migration

While reviewing my notes for this book in April 2007, I saw where I had written the Bible verses, Genesis 2:6 and 2:10. Of particular interest was the reference to "water" as a key word in both verses. The verses read respectively, "But there went up a mist from the earth, and watered the whole face of the ground" and "And a river went out of Eden to water the garden and from thence it was parted, and became into four heads."

On Labor Day 2006, it was revealed that the phrase, "to water the garden," in Genesis 2:10 meant Eve was pregnant when she and Adam were banished from the Garden of Eden. At the time, I had not interpreted the phrase "watered the whole face of the ground."

I now believe that the definition of the word "ground" as mentioned in Genesis 2:5, "...there was not a man to till the ground," refers metaphorically to the "ground" being akin to a woman's womb. When I combine the meanings of the word "ground," which refers to a woman's womb and "water," which refers to pregnancy and a woman in labor, I conclude Genesis 2:6, "watered the whole face of the ground," metaphorically means God created man from the "ground" or the "dust."

Also, notice the similarity of the phrases "watered the whole face of the ground" that appears in Genesis 2:6 and "to water the garden [a piece of ground]" in Genesis 2:10. Both phrases are referring to watering the ground. These findings strengthen my belief that Eve was pregnant and would soon go into labor when she and Adam were banished from the Garden of Eden.

In order for the interpretation of scripture about the story of the first man on earth to be credible, there must be answers to the questions "who, what, where, when and how." On April 17, 2007, the missing piece to the story of the first man was revealed. The answer to "who" is Adam. The answer to "what" is his creation. The answer to "where" is Ethiopia. The answer to "when" is thousands of years ago as noted by dated fossils. And, the answer to "how" is from the dust of the earth. Yes, we all know that Adam, the first man was created from the dust of the earth because that's how the scripture reads. I sought proof by using the "defined word approach."

Remember, two paragraphs earlier, I wrote that I now believe Genesis 2:6, "watered the whole face of the ground," metaphorically refers to God creating man from the dust of the ground. Interestingly, in the *Random House Unabridged Dictionary*, a synonym for "face" is "appearance," which is archaically defined as an apparition. The dictionary defines "apparition" as anything that appears in an extraordinary way; especially a figure appearing suddenly and thought to be a ghost.

This definition of "apparition" spurs my conclusion that Genesis 2:6 is describing the creation of the first man. Genesis 2:7, which follows, reads; "And the Lord God formed man of the dust of the ground, and breathed into his nostrils the breath of life; and man became a living soul."

To further strengthen my hypothesis regarding man's creation, a synonym for "apparition" is "spirit," which the dictionary defines as the life principle, especially in human beings, originally regarded as inherent in the breath or as infused by a deity. In short, we have a series of words by themselves, which may not always seem related, but actually tie into each other in a biblical context that describes the creation of mankind.

The reader may ask, from whence did these other people come? According to Genesis 2:1, it appears when God created Adam he also created other people. The verse reads, "Thus the heavens and the earth were finished, all the hosts of them." The key words found in the verse appear in the phrase "all the host[s]." The word "host" is defined as "a multitude or a large number." The key word in the definition of "host" is "multitude." The word "multitude" preceded by the word "all" indicates many people were created shortly after Adam. While a "multitude" of people were created, the Bible's story focuses on Adam's lineage and specifi-cally, the bloodline that led to the birth of Jesus Christ.

****

I believe the answer to Adam's origin may be buried in one of the many definitions of the word "east." Ironically, the word "east" is emblazoned on the wall of the building where the offices of W.J. Alexander & Associates' office are located. Since Janu-ary 2002, I had looked at the word "east" each day upon entering or leaving the building. That word, as I would eventually learn, was a major clue to the unsolved mystery regarding Adam and Eve's origin.

Based on my research using the "defined word approach," I believe man was created in Ethiopia and migrated to the Garden of Eden.

As mentioned in Chapter 6, The Truth Shall Rise, I originally thought one of the definitions of the word "east" meant someone leaving Ethiopia. The OED's Second Edition,[28] Volume V, page 36, defines the word "east" as an adverb: "With reference to motion or position: In the direction of the part of the horizon where the sun rises. More definitely: In the direction of that point of the horizon which is 90° to the right of the north point; also due east." This definition of the word "east" appears to serve as a map, providing directions from Ethiopia to the Garden of Eden. I believe the definition could also be describing Adam and Eve leaving Ethiopia, traveling to a northern point on the horizon and from there, traveling toward the sunrise to ultimately end their journey in the Garden of Eden.

I reached this conclusion by analyzing the aforementioned adverbial quotation, which defines the word "east." The following is my analysis: With "reference to motion," describes Adam and Eve leaving Ethiopia. Also, "In the direction of the part of the horizon where the sun rises," is indicating Adam and Eve headed in an eastern direction. The second part of the definition, "More definitely: in the direction of that point of the horizon which is 90° to the right of the north point," is reconfirming that Adam and Eve left Ethiopia, reached a northern point in their journey, then headed east.

The preceding assumption is also based on my study of the World Atlas map of northeastern Africa and the Middle East, with specific interest in the locations of Ethiopia and the small part of modern-day Iraq commonly identified as the approximate site of the Garden of Eden as it appears on ancient biblical maps. The map of northeastern Africa is shown on *the color plate insert* as it appears in the Great World Atlas and other publications. If you drew an imaginary line on this map of northeastern Africa going north from Ethiopia, it reaches a point where the Garden of Eden is located 90° to the east of this point.

Upon reading this description found in the definition of "east" and looking at the map of northeastern Africa, it appears that in order to describe the preceding directions in the 14th century, one would have traveled in the region in which the directions are charted. If the original author never actually visited the region, this might suggest some sort of divine intervention similar to what Moses wrote in the Bible's book of Job 26:7: "God stretches the northern sky over empty space and hangs the earth on nothing." In my view, the use of the word "northern" in this verse closely resembles the language in the OED's definition of the word "east."

According to the *King James Version Hebrew-Greek Key Word Study Bible*, on page 669, "Although there is no mention of the author's name within the book [of Job], most scholars accept the Talmudic tradition that Moses is the author of the book." It should be noted of course, that Moses is also widely believed to be the author of the book of Genesis. In the book of Genesis, Moses writes about the accounts of the first man and woman on earth. This is another indication, in my view, that Moses had to have had divine guidance in writing in detail about people like Adam and Eve who lived over 100,000 years before his existence.

The word "north" being so prominently mentioned in defining the word "east" brings to mind the word "compass." A "compass" is defined as "an instrument for determining directions, as by means of a freely rotating magnetized needle that indicates magnetic north." I wondered if there was a connection.

In the book, *The Travels of Sir John Mandeville*, which was written around 1357, Ethiopia is discussed in detail. In another one of the OED's definitions of "east," the quotation, "Ethiope is departed" is attributed to the author and oceanographer, Sir John Mandeville. Originally, in looking at one of the many definitions of the word, "east," the quotation "Ethiope is departed" appeared to mean someone had left one point en route to another point. I would later learn that the word "departed" translates to mean "divided." However, my initial interpretation of the word, "departed," led me to take a closer look at routes in this region.

I later learned "Ethiope is departed," is properly translated to mean "Ethiopia is divided" — meaning split into eastern and southern regions. Although, I had originally misinterpreted the meaning of "departed," ultimately the word "departed" led me to think in terms of geographical locations. If I had understood the word to mean "divided," I doubt I would have ever been persuaded to look at a map. When I first read this quotation, I literally interpreted "departed" in its modern meaning, as in someone having left one point en route to another.

In *The Travels of Sir John Mandeville,* it is clear that Mandeville presented an accurate description of travel routes in

Ethiopia and the Holy Land, which encompasses the Garden of Eden.

The King James Version of the Holy Bible — which was written more than 254 years after *The Travels of Sir John Mandeville*—first mentions Ethiopia in Genesis 2:13. I believe the word "compasseth" in verse 13 may reveal Adam and Eve walking along the banks of the Nile River inside of Ethiopia. After leaving Ethiopia, they continued walking along the Nile in the direction of the Garden of Eden. There are some similarities between my personal scenario and the one presented in the documentary *"The Real Eve"* concerning what provoked Adam and Eve's migration from Ethiopia to the Garden of Eden.

My personal scenario of Adam and Eve leaving Ethiopia was developed while pursuing the definition of key words — "compasseth" and "Gihon" in Genesis 2:13. The verse reads, "And the name of the second river is Gihon: the same is it that compasseth the whole land of Ethiopia."

The definition of the word, "compasseth," is located in the Key Word Study Bible. It is identified by the number 5437 and found on page 76 in the Key Word Study Bible reference section titled, Greek Dictionary of the New Testament. According to the dictionary's explanation, the number 5437 indicates the corresponding Hebrew word appears in Strong's Concordance, a biblical dictionary.

The Hebrew word for "compasseth" is "phuge," which means fleeing. The examples used for fleeing are "escape" or "flight." It is also noted the word "phuge," is represented by the number 5343 — and comes from the word, "pheugo," a primary verb which means to "run away" (literally or figuratively); by implication "to shun;" by analogy, "to vanish;" or to "escape, flee" (away). The word "pheugo" and its definition are found on page 75 in the same section as the word, "phuge."

The other key word in Genesis 2:13, "Gihon," is referring to a river well known by another name, Nile River. The Nile River has a branch, the Blue Nile, which flows out of Ethiopia in a south to north direction. The river flows down hill, from the high mountains of Ethiopia in the middle of Africa to the Nile delta, which is the point where the Nile River flows into the Mediterranean Sea.

Like the Wise Men who followed the star as a compass in their search for the baby Jesus (Matthew 2:2), I believe Adam and Eve used the banks of the Nile River as their compass. They left Ethiopia due to a famine or some other disaster, walked along the river banks and followed its downhill pathway toward the Mediterranean Sea. This migratory route would have taken them to the Sinai Peninsula. From there, they walked the same path the children of Israel would later follow as they fled Egypt going through what would become the Promised Land and on to the Garden of Eden. Later, their descendants left the Garden of Eden and walked to Yemen as hypothesized in *"The Real Eve"* documentary.

****

A close examination of the word "Easter," which is rooted in the word "east," may reveal the continued migration of man from the Garden of Eden to the Far East. As mentioned earlier, the word "east," in a biblical context, refers to the direction Adam and Eve followed in finding the Garden of Eden. When you add the suffix "er," to the definition of "east" it seems to suggest moving in an "eastern" direction. Among many of the definitions of "er," two are of interest. One definition defines the word as "from their place or origin or abode" and the other defines the word as "a termination of nouns denoting action or process." These two definitions of "er" heavily reinforced my thinking that Adam and Eve were moving toward an "eastern" destination and man traveled farther "east."

According to *"The Real Eve,"* Eve's descendants left Ethiopia due to a famine destroying food sources in their homeland. The documentary tells the story of how her descendants crossed the Persian Gulf during a period when the water level was very low. Supposedly, they walked on sandbars to cross over to Yemen and continued their southbound journey to Australia up to the Far East. My scenario and the documentary's scenario ultimately arrive at the same conclusion about the destination of Eve's descendants, with the key difference being in the routes taken.

The Eve documentary further enhances my theory. It also tells the story of the earliest modern human skull found in sediment in a cave dating back 120,000 years. Human bones were found near Nazareth in Galilee in 1933. There were 13 fragile skeletons, including one of a woman with the skeleton of a tiny baby at her feet. These were the oldest complete modern human skeletons ever found. The numerous skeletons found in caves in Israel shows there were modern humans outside of Africa more than 100,000 years ago. It is thought man may have gone up the

Nile corridor through Sinai into the Middle East.

Both scenarios of Adam and Eve leaving Ethiopia are plausible since there are biblical stories regarding famines uprooting families. Joseph rose to prominence in Egypt when he warned the pharaoh of the coming famine (Genesis 41:27). During the time Abraham lived in Canaan, there was a famine. He moved with his wife, Sarai, to Egypt and waited for the famine to end (Genesis 12:10). Jacob sent 10 of his sons to Egypt in search of food due to a famine in Canaan (Genesis 42:2-3).

Thousands of years later in the United States, Abraham Lincoln signed the Emancipation Proclamation that freed the slaves. Blacks would exodus the South in several waves, over the course of nearly one hundred years, for a better life in the North. These southern blacks were fleeing what amounted to a kind of modern-day "famine" — economic poverty and legally enforced racial discrimination. Their travel routes would take them along the roads pointing north. Specifically, many blacks left Mississippi on roads heading toward Northern or Midwestern cities like St. Louis and Chicago. Simultaneously, many blacks were leaving Alabama, traveling through Tennessee and Kentucky, en route to Gary, Indiana, Detroit, Cleveland and other cities in the north to find a new way of life. Throughout the better part of the 20th century, blacks used these routes, which later became highways, and many others to leave the south in search of better living standards.

****

In the case of Adam and Eve's origin, in order to have a

believable location for the creation of man, there are certain things that need to be in place. When God created them, it is conceivable, they were naked. Therefore, the environmental conditions had to be suitable for the survival of a naked person. In order to have a believable place for man to be created, the area's climate had to be like an incubator that would have allowed him to survive as a naked person in the conditions of the environment. Thus, Adam and Eve being created in Ethiopia make sense. The daytime temperature in southern Ethiopia located near the equator— *as shown on the map in the color plate insert*—is a high of 122° and a night-time low of 81°. Common sense dictates that a man could survive and live in Ethiopia's hot climate without clothing.

****

I would like to make one final comment on this topic. Shortly after returning from my visit in Atlanta, my friend there sent me a magazine article titled "The Greatest Journey Ever Told, The Trail of Our DNA." The article was published in *National Geographic*[29] and dated March 2006. It talks about people genes tracing back to Africa and from there traveling around the world. It states, "Homo sapiens, or modern humans, headed east from Africa as long as 70,000 years ago — Scientists now calculate that all living humans are related to a single woman who lived roughly 150,000 years ago in Africa, a 'mitochondrial Eve.'"

Chapter 9 - Adam's Skin Color

In proceeding from my belief that Adam's place of origin was Ethiopia, I am making the following assertions using what I call the "defined word approach," which I introduced in Chapter 5. This "approach" enabled me to interpret Genesis 2:12, which reads, "and the gold of that land is good: there is bdellium and the onyx stone." I believe the definition of the key word, "gold," describes Adam as "uncivilized" — or uncultured. And the key words "bdellium" and "onyx" describe Adam as a man with black skin.

The following clarifies how these conclusions about Adam were reached. Using the "defined word approach," an Old and Middle English cognate in Webster's definition of "gold" on page 819 links the words, "gold" and "goth." The word "goth," found on page 825 of the same dictionary, is defined as "a person of no refinement; barbarian." It makes sense. If Adam was the first man created, he would be uncivilized — as there was no civilization and no social mores. If uncivilized, he would fit the description of a barbarian — "a person in a savage, primitive state; uncivilized person."

A seminal event in the evolution of man occurs in Genesis 3:7. It reads, "And the eyes of them both were opened, and they knew that they were naked; and they sewed fig leaves together, and made themselves aprons. The key words are "apron" and "fig leaf." Webster's define "apron" as an article of apparel covering part of the front of the body and tied at the waist. In the case of Adam and Eve, the apron would hide their genitalia. This is noted by the reference to "fig leaf," which Webster's define as a representation of such a leaf used, as in sculpture, to conceal the genitals of a nude or anything intended to conceal. The wearing of an "apron" indicates Adam and Eve after committing the original sins became conscious of their bodies for the first time. Thus man began to wear clothing.

There is further proof of Adam and Eve's evolution and barbaric nature, as documented in a later time period, specifically, the story of Lot and his daughters. Lot and his family were barbarians, as noted by the Bible's mention of their home being a cave (Genesis 19:30). On the other hand, Noah's father, Lamech married Adah, who gave birth to their son Jabal, who was the first to live in a tent (Genesis 4:20). This is an indication that man was evolving out of his barbaric state.

With this knowledge of Adam's culture, his first time wearing clothes and their housing, let's look at what's said about his skin color. The dictionary's definitions of key words, "bdellium," and "onyx" were not helpful. In fact, when I first read the definition of the word "bdellium," it led me to think of gum or resin. However, the OED's following Middle English quotations provided much needed insight after being interpreted. They read: 1) "Bidellium is..a blacke tre moost lyke to the Oliue and the gumme therof is bright and bytter." 2) "The Man also was..the colour of bdellium."

I called on a professor at a local university to interpret these Middle English quotations into Modern English. When translated into Modern English, quotation one reads; "Bdellium is a black (or dark) tree, very similar to the Olive tree, and the sap [or gum] of the bdellium is shining and bitter." When translated to Modern English,* quotation two reads; "The man also was the color [black] of bdellium."

In these quotations, I think the Bible is using the word "tree" metaphorically as "applied figuratively or **allusively** to a person." While interpreting Genesis 2:9 – "And the Lord God planted all sorts of trees in the garden," I thought the "tree" referred meta-phorically to a man. The quotation, which refers to bdellium as a black tree and the man being the color of bdellium, gives credibil-ity to thinking metaphorically of the tree as being a black person.

The word "onyx" is further defined by its usage in the OED's quotation; "The Indian Onyx hath certaine sparkes in it … As for the Arabian Onyches, there bee found of them blacke, with white circles." When translated to Modern English, the quotation reads; The onyx of India has special sparks (fiery particles) in it…As for the onyxes of Arabia, there are black varieties, with white circles. I think the notable part of this quotation is the words, "black vari-eties with white circles."

We will later learn in the chapter "Miscegenation," how the once divided black and white family of Abra**ham** reunites. The divided families were those of Shem, represented by his descen-dant Judah and **Ham** represented by his descendant Tamar. These families, which had parted ways, were reunited like the colors of the onyx stone. I believe the "onyx stone" is a metaphor repre-

Note: While speaking to another professor at the local black university, it was interesting to learn that black people in general do not attend college and study to become medievalists. As the professor said, "Why would you major in a subject knowing you probably won't find a job after graduating?"

senting the unification of these formerly divided families.

I also believe the onyx stone symbolizes the families of Noah's sons, Shem and Ham, unifying when Jacob's son, Judah, fathered Pharez as a result of his tryst with Tamar, the Canaanite. The onyx stone also symbolizes the interracial marriages that took place during the children of Israel's captivity in Egypt. An example of interracial marriage, while in captivity, would be Moses marrying an Ethiopian [black] woman (Numbers 12:1). Oddly, the Key Word Study Bible defines the word "woman" but not the word "Ethiopian." Even when the word "Ethiopian" is used as an adjective to describe "woman," it is not defined. Both words, which are found in Numbers 12:1 read; "And Miriam and Aaron spake against Moses because of the Ethiopian woman who he had married: for he had married an Ethiopian woman."

It appears Miriam and Aaron were concerned about Moses marrying an individual who was not an Egyptian. Could this be the first written account regarding an interracial marriage? This scripture leads me to believe Numbers 12:1 also confirms black descendants of Ham were held captive in Egypt, during the 400 years, along with Abraham's descendants.

Of specific interest was the "Superior Roman Numeral" that is found in the Key Word Study Bible in front of the word "Ethiopia" and other words in the Bible. I was told during a telephone conversation by a representative of the Key Word Study Bible's publishing company that the Superior Roman Numeral is designed to be a help and the words so noted in the Bible are not considered inspired scripture.

The word "Ethiopia" is written in a minimum of 20 Bible

verses and "Ethiopian," seven. While they may not be words inspired by scripture, the words denote factually that Ethiopia and Ethiopians were significant in biblical history.

****

The Bible tells the story of the Tower of Babel. At this time in history, I believe the families of Shem, Ham and Japheth were all the same skin color (Genesis 11:1-9). The first verse reads; the whole world "spoke a single language" and "used the same words." The key word is "language." Webster's defines "language" as "a body of words and the systems for their use common to a people who are of the same community or nation, the same geographical area, or the same cultural tradition."

It appears that at the Tower of Babel, mankind had reached a point where people began to develop different beliefs. The logical next step would be their going separate ways.

Another key word is "geographical," which is defined as "of or pertaining to geography." According to Webster's, "geography' is defined as the science dealing with the areal [aerial] differentiation of the earth's surface, as shown in the character, arrangement, and interrelations over the world of such elements as climate, elevation, soil, vegetation, population." By scattering the people to different "geographical" regions, which had different climates, the skin color would naturally change after years of living in a warm, cold or hot region.

When God scattered the people, I believe Shem's family stayed in the Middle East, Ham's family migrated back to sub-

Saharan Africa and Japheth's family migrated to Germany and Russia. Others continued their migratory routes that eventually led to the Far East and on to America. The Tower of Babel symbolizes the first creation of the races. People who were once united singularly in appearance and language became separated as a result of God's will.

****

Friday morning, January 26, 2007, I was pondering the previous day's discovery of Adam's skin color as that of a black man. I wondered how the color "black," created by God, could come to depict so many negative connotations. For me, the calm of early morning darkness always initiated the start of my day. My daily morning walk has been perfect for getting my thought process started. There I am, walking in the early morning darkness, which offers a sense of serenity required for the awakening of my thought process. To me, the beauty of darkness symbolizes a time for prayer, meditation, thinking, or simple reflection on inner thoughts — all of which prove useful in writing this book.

With minimum distractions, the darkness lighted by the stars, moon, street lights, and an occasional front porch light created the perfect ambiance. The light combined with the darkness reminded me of an onyx stone and its perfect combination of black and white.

****

Dr. Martin Luther King Jr., in his book, *Where Do We Go from Here?*, carefully detailed how words like "black" and "dark" have long been used to describe unpleasant people, places and things. He also notes Ossie Davis' views on how these negative connotations *affect a black child's self-image* in the formative years. Dr. King's reference to "black" and "dark" in his book reads:

Even semantics have conspired to make that which is black seem ugly and degrading. In Roget's Thesaurus, there are 120 synonyms for blackness and at least 60 of them are offensive, as for example, blot, soot, grim, devil and foul. And there are some 134 synonyms for whiteness and all are favorable, expressed in such words as purity, cleanliness, chastity and innocence. A white lie is better than a black lie. The most degenerate member of a family is a black sheep. Ossie Davis has suggested that maybe, the English language should be reconstructed so that teachers will not be forced to teach the Negro child 60 ways to despise himself, and thereby perpetuate his false sense of inferiority, and the white child 134 ways to adore himself, and thereby perpetuate his false sense of superiority."

As we read their words today, it is clear that Dr. King and his friend, Ossie Davis, both understood the destructive power of misused words like "darkness." They also could see the tragedy of *failing to challenge the misuse* of those words.

****

In September 2006, Kiri Davis, a 17-year-old high school filmmaker, once again stirred up the debate over skin color in her eight-minute video involving black and white dolls. Davis was doing her own version of an experiment conducted in 1954 by Kenneth B. Clark, a black psychologist. Black dolls and white dolls were shown to small black children to see which of the dolls were considered prettier and which were considered good and evil. Davis, the young filmmaker, got the same results Clark did 50 years earlier. Specifically, the small black children overwhelmingly chose the white dolls as the prettiest and the nicest.

Almost 15 years before the Supreme Court heard the Brown v. Board of Education case, Dr. Clark's wife, Mamie, was working on her master's degree thesis. Her research showed that "black children often preferred to play with white dolls over black." The black children would fill in the color of a lighter shade rather than their own color when asked to color human figures. The children's mindset equated being black as ugly and white, pretty. In the Clarks' minds, they saw this as evidence of internalized racism caused by stigmatization.

The results of Clark's experiment served as evidence in the Brown v. Board of Education case and were largely considered to be conclusive evidence of segregation's impact on the self-image of young black children. Kiri Davis' documentary reveals little has changed regarding black children's self-image since the days of Clark's experiment.

What goes unsaid is what happened to the children in the

1954 experiment and other black children who thought like them who grew to adulthood. In 1968, Dr. Martin Luther King, Jr. in his last recorded speech told the people he saw the Promised Land and thus a brighter day. The Godfather of Soul, James Brown, in lyrics encouraged the people to, "Say It Loud — I'm Black And I'm Proud." And the legendary soul singers, The Impressions, followed up with their hit single, "We're A Winner." Dr. King's words and these songs of pride were all attempts to instill pride in a fragile black psyche.

Sadly, these attempts failed to reach many in the black community. This was poignantly revealed by Destiny's Child singer Kelly Rowland. In a July 27, 2007, Houston Chronicle article, Rowland revealed that she once wished she was more fair-skinned. Rowland added, "But Tina Knowles, Beyonce's mom, would say, 'Don't you know how beautiful you are?' She made me come into my brown beauty."

Chapter 10 – Noah Curses Canaan

Why such an interest in the biblical story of Noah cursing Canaan, his grandson and the son of Ham? This story is relevant because, as the LASB footnote on page 20 reads, Genesis 9:25 "has been wrongfully used to support racial prejudice and even slavery. Noah's curse, however, wasn't directed toward any particular race, but rather at the Canaanite nation — a nation God knew would become wicked. The curse was fulfilled when the Israelites entered the Promised Land and drove the Canaanites out."

If the scripture said the curse was fulfilled then that's believable. If a biblical scholar says the curse was fulfilled, that's debatable. I question when the curse was fulfilled as noted by the biblical scholars.

Since spring 2006, I have been reading and trying to interpret Genesis 9:25 and the surrounding verses. In my view, the fact that the LASB's authors deemed it necessary to add a special footnote for the verses detailing Noah's curse against Canaan, indicates those authors understood the historical significance of the curse.

The authors of the Key Word Study Bible also offer an explanation regarding Ham's actions and Noah cursing Canaan in a footnote on page 16. Their explanation reads, "The statement in verse twenty-two that Ham was the father of Canaan, and the fact that Noah's curse is directed against Canaan (v. 25) indicate that Canaan was somehow involved in immoral and indecent behavior with his drunken grandfather." The footnote continues; "Ham was indirectly to blame because he had allowed Canaan to grow up with this character and because he evidently did not treat Noah with respect when he found him."

It would be interesting to understand the process used to determine *how* the scholars concluded Canaan was involved in immoral and indecent behavior. I respectfully disagree with the biblical scholars.

In February 2007, I decided to reread the chapter, "From Ham to Canaan" found in the late Dr. George O. McCalep Jr.'s book, *When Black Men Stretch Their Hands to God*. In this chapter, Dr. McCalep writes about his research of this well-known biblical curse. He discusses the interpretation of the curse as put forth by Rev. Dwight McKissic, who, along with other theologians and biblical scholars, "disagree with the scriptural interpretation that Canaan had sex with his grandmother." Based on research, scripture interpretation and discernment, I agree that Canaan did not have sex with his grandmother.

The Bible verse to which McKissic refers is Genesis 9:23. Before proceeding with my interpretation of this verse and its surrounding verses, I think it is important to review the full story. Noah's curse on Canaan takes place after the Great Flood and begins in Genesis 9:18:

*And the sons of Noah, that went forth of the ark, were Shem, and Ham, and Japheth: and **Ham is the father of Canaan**. [19] These are the three sons of Noah: and* *of them was the whole earth overspread. [20] And Noah began to be a husbandman, and he planted a vineyard: [21] And he drank of the wine, and was drunken; and he **was uncovered within his tent**. [22] "And **Ham, the father of Canaan, saw the nakedness of his father, and told his two brethren without.** [23] And Shem and Japheth took a garment, and laid it upon both their shoulders, and went backward, and covered the nakedness of their father; and their faces were backward, **and they saw not their father's nakedness**. [24] And Noah awoke from his wine, and **knew** what his younger son had done unto him. [25] And he said, **Cursed be Canaan; a servant of servants shall he be unto his brethren.** [26] And he said, Blessed be the LORD God of Shem; **and Canaan shall be his servant.** [27] God shall enlarge Japheth, and he shall dwell in the tents of Shem; and **Canaan shall be his servant.**" [28] And Noah lived after the flood three hundred and fifty years. [29] And all the days of Noah were nine hundred and fifty years: and he died.*

(Key words in the verses have been intentionally bolded because I will refer back to them frequently while interpreting.) After the Great Flood, Noah and his wife and his sons and their wives left the ark, started new lives and started repopulating the world. In Noah's case, it appears he started a new career as a winemaker.

Based on the information provided by Dr. McCalep and

information that follows, I do not believe Noah's wife was Shem, Ham and Japheth's maternal mother.

An indication that Noah's wife was not their maternal mother appears in Genesis 7:7 and 7:13. The first verse reads: "And he [Noah] went aboard the boat to escape — he [Noah] and his wife and his sons [Shem, Ham and Japheth] and their wives."

The second verse reads: "But Noah had gone into the boat that very day with his wife and his sons [Shem, Ham and Japheth] and their wives." Note the sentence structure that twice separates Noah's relationship with his wife from the relationship with his sons. There is no suggestion that this wife is the mother of Noah's sons Shem, Ham and Japheth.

As the story goes, one day Noah drank wine he made in his vineyard and got drunk. In order to understand what may have happened afterward, I first use the LASB's cross references to this story. Cross referencing involves one or more verses sharing a similar meaning or context with another. The verse that follows Genesis 9:21 where Noah drank the wine reads; "And Ham, the father of Canaan, saw the nakedness of his father, and told his two brethren without." While it is clear from this verse that Ham is the father of Canaan, there's no apparent mention of Canaan's mother. Or is there?

Cross reference Genesis 9:22 to Habakkuk 2:15 to Hosea 7:5 which reads, "On royal holidays, the princes get drunk. The king makes a fool of himself and drinks with those who are making fun of him." This verse leads me to believe Noah got drunk in the company of his sons and became a source of entertainment for them. He drank too much, ended up in a drunken stupor and fell asleep in his tent. My interpretation of the aforementioned scripture implies Noah's son Ham, after discovering Noah had passed out, used the opportunity to violate him. This is also indicated by the phrase in verse 9:21, "uncovered within his tent," which I believe means Ham made no attempt to hide his actions from his drunken father.

Genesis 9:21 cross references Habakkuk 2:15, which reads; "How terrible it will be for you who make your neighbors drunk! You force your cup on them so that you can gloat over their nakedness and shame." This verse implies getting another drunk in order to take advantage of his degraded state. "Gloating," which means "to gaze or think with exultation or malicious pleasure," leads me to think of someone enjoying the fact that his victim is present and unaware of what is being done against him.

Dr. McCalep mentions the following story about Lot and his two daughters on page 59 in his book. You may recall that this story was referenced in Chapter 6 of this book. It bears repeating because it appeared in the book, *Travels of Sir John Mandeville* 250 years before it was written in the KJV Holy Bible. The cross reference that leads to Lot's story is Genesis 9:21. It reads, "One day he became drunk on some wine he had made and lay naked in his tent." The story of Lot and his daughters is found in Genesis 19:30-38. The daughters plotted to get their father drunk and have sex with him without his knowledge to preserve their family line. The older daughter had a son who was the ancestor of the Moabites and the younger daughter's son was the ancestor of the Ammonites. The fact that Genesis 9:21 — with its discussion of Noah's drinking — is a cross reference to Genesis

19:35, implies Ham got Noah drunk in order to take advantage of Noah's wife *in a manner similar to what Lot experienced* with his daughters.

Like Moabites and Ammonites resulted from the incestuous encounter between Lot and his daughters, a child named Canaan, the father of the Canaanites, may have been conceived from the incestuous relationship between Noah's son, Ham, and Noah's wife. In this cross reference story there is an apparent theme of incest. The combination of this cross reference story and the "defined word approach" that I have used provides insight into unraveling the mystery of Noah, his son Ham and grandson Canaan.

As written in Genesis 9:22, "Ham ... saw the nakedness of his father..." The aforementioned biblical verse, Genesis 9:22, the cross reference verses and Dr. McCalep's scripture notation of Leviticus 20:11 that follows leads me to believe that Ham had intercourse with his father's wife. Dr. McCalep elaborates about the "father's nakedness" on pages 58 and 59 in his book, which leads me to my conclusion. He writes:

> *Father's nakedness described 'sexual intercourse.' Leviticus 20:11 reads: 'And the man that lieth with his father's wife hath uncovered his father's nakedness: both of them shall surely be put to death; their blood shall be upon them.'" Dr. McCalep goes on to write, "According to this Scripture, when a son had sex with his father's wife, he uncovered his father's nakedness. Deuteronomy 27:20 says, "Cursed be he that lieth with*

his father's wife; because he uncovereth his father's skirt. And all the people shall say, Amen.

But how is this so? Remember, in the previous chapter, I talked about Adam and Eve, and that Eve was pulled from Adam's rib, and Adam declared that Eve was flesh of his flesh and bone of his bone. Eve's body was a part of Adam's body. Paul said in Ephesians 5:33, "Nevertheless let every one of you in particular so love his wife even as himself; and the wife see that she reverence her husband." This Scripture tell us that men are to love their wives just as they love their own bodies, which mean that the wife's body is a part of the husband's. Therefore, if a man has sex with someone else's wife, then he has uncovered her husband's nakedness.

In Genesis 9:24, after Noah awakens, he slowly gains knowledge of what Ham has done. Webster's defines the present tense of "knew," which is the word "know" as "to perceive or understand as fact or truth; to apprehend clearly and with certainty." The verse tells us through the use of the word "know," that Noah has become alert to how Ham has violated him. The knowledge may have been: 1) Noah catching Ham in the act; 2) Ham mocking his father by telling him of his actions; or 3) The other two brothers telling Noah.

This narrative by Dr. McCalep regarding, "Saw the nakedness of his father," also answers the question of whether

Canaan's mother was ever specifically identified. As shown below, "father's nakedness" refers to Noah's wife.

Dr. McCalep's writings indicate 1) "Nakedness" refers to the behavior of Noah's wife; 2) His research also reaffirms my belief that Ham had intercourse with his father's wife, an act which I believe the Bible points out by using the phrase, "uncovered his father's nakedness."

On page 60 of his book, Dr. McCalep notes the Rev. Dwight McKissic's contention that "There is nothing in the interpretation of Hebrew Scripture that links 'seeing' in Genesis 9:23 where Ham 'saw the nakedness of his father' with a sexual act. Therefore, sexual activity is unrelated to whatever may have happened."

I disagree with Rev. McKissic's interpretation as it relates to the word "saw" and no sexual activity being associated with the phrase, "saw the nakedness of his father." The Key Word Study Bible defines the word "saw," which is found on page 1658 and noted by the number "7200," as "to know." The word "know," archaically defined means, "to have sexual intercourse with."

I also contend that if scholars translated the original biblical manuscript to English correctly, the word "saw" in its present tense "see" also has a sexual connotation. Webster's defines the word, "see," as "to court, keep company with, or date frequently." The etymology of the word "see" is 900 A.D. This date is important because the word's origin is before the writing of the Holy Bible KJV.

I agreed earlier with Rev. McKissic and other theologians that Canaan did not have sex with his grandmother. However, as previously mentioned, I think Ham did have a "tryst" with his step-mother. Here's the continuation of the scenario. While Ham's father was in a drunken stupor, Ham "saw the nakedness of his father." After engaging in consensual sex with his stepmother, Ham tells his brothers. This is noted by the phrase, "told his two brethren without." In this scenario, Ham's brothers, Shem and Japheth, were outside the tent at the time of the incident.

Shem and Japheth not seeing "their father's nakedness" implies them not being aware of their brother, Ham's affair with their stepmother, Noah's wife. After telling his brothers, the two brothers tried to keep their father from finding out. This is noted by Shem and Japheth "covering the nakedness of their father." Webster's defines "cover" as "to hide the wrongful or embarrassing action of another by providing an alibi."

As Dr. McCalep said regarding the interpretation that Canaan had sex with his grandmother, "How awful!" On this point, I agree with Dr. McCalep. Personally, I believe it is repugnant and immoral for any person to engage in sexual intercourse with any blood relative. But what I am saying about Canaan is that he did nothing to bring on the curse. It was his father, Ham, who engaged in a sexual relationship with his stepmother who later gave birth to Canaan. Ultimately, Canaan was punished for his father's sin.

Dr. McCalep writes about other theologian's interpreta-tions of Noah cursing Canaan in his book, *When Black Men Stretch Their Hands to God — Messages Affirming The Biblical Black Heritage*.[30] He writes none of them explain why Canaan was cursed and Ham was not:

Biblical historian Josephus said "Noah did not curse Ham by reason of his nearness in blood, but cursed his posterity."

A theologian, Arthur C. Custance contends Noah could not pronounce judgment of any kind upon his son, Ham, the actual offender, without passing judgment upon himself, for society held him, the father, responsible for his son's behavior. To punish Ham, then, he must of necessity pronounce a curse upon Canaan, Ham's son.

A Canadian writer named Carlisle John Peterson says "Ham was not cursed, but his son Canaan was. He writes, "when the son of man in covenant with God violates his covenantal duty, that son does not experience the consequence of his transgression in his lifetime, but his son experiences the consequences of his father's violation of the covenant."

The question remains, why did the Lord allow the curse on Canaan? I believe the curse is a continuation of a series of events signaling the coming of Jesus Christ. It appears, for example, that the curse on Canaan does the same and was preordained in Genesis 5:28-29. The verses read, "And Lamech lived a hundred eighty and two years, and begat a son: and he called his name Noah, saying, This same shall comfort us concerning our work and toil of our hands, because of the ground which the Lord hath cursed." God cursed Adam and Eve saying "Because thou hast ... eaten of the tree, of which I commanded thee, saying Thou shalt not eat of it: cursed is the ground for thy sake; in sorrow shalt thou eat of it all the days of thy life" (Genesis 3:17).

As previously stated, Noah's father, Lamech, says in Genesis 5:29, his son, Noah will bring relief. Genesis 5:29 cross references back to Genesis 3:17 where God cursed Adam and Eve. Before interpreting 3:17, I think an interpretation of Genesis 3:14 will assist with the interpretation of 3:17. Genesis 3:14 reads; "And the LORD God said unto the serpent, Because thou hast done this, thou art cursed above all cattle, and above every beast of the field; upon thy belly shalt thou go, and dust shalt thou eat all the days of thy life."

In this verse, I believe God curses the "serpent" for seducing Eve. I interpreted the "serpent" to be a man. One of the definitions of "serpent" is a "wily, treacherous, or malicious person." I believe when God proclaimed the "serpent" is cursed above the "cattle" and every "beast," he is referring to "cattle" as disparaging human beings and "beast" refers to men who are cruel, coarse and filthy or otherwise beastlike people. Remember, we are talking about the first people on earth.

Even the reference to "belly" denotes a man. "Belly" is defined as the "lower front part of the human body between the chest and thighs." A definition of "dust" describes it with the phrase, "lick the dust," which means to be "servile; grovel." The word "servile" has an archaic meaning that refers to being "held in slavery." The word "grovel" means "to behave humbly or abjectly, as before authority; debase oneself in a servile fashion, to wallow in what is low or contemptible." I dare ask; could the serpent's curse be the foretelling of slavery?

Genesis 3:17 reads; "And unto Adam he said, Because thou

hast hearkened unto the voice of thy wife, and hast eaten of the tree, of which I commanded thee, saying, Thou shalt not eat of it: cursed is the ground for thy sake, in sorrow shalt thou eat of it all the days of thy life."

Here it is noted in Genesis 3:17 that Adam and Eve and their descendants were cursed and would have to scratch a living from the ground as noted, "cursed is the ground for thy sake." I believe Adam and Eve were cursed because Eve allowed herself to be seduced by the serpent. She convinced Adam to do the same. I interpret the original sin as Adam and Eve committing adultery. For their sin, they were banished from the Garden of Eden and God cursed the ground against all mankind. I will elaborate on this subject in the Epilogue.

I believe the relief referred to by Lamech starts when Noah curses the descendants of Canaan. The sexual relationship between Tamar, the Canaanite, and Judah, the Semite, conceived Pharez, who was a direct ancestor of Jesus Christ. Christians believe Jesus died on the cross for all the sins of the world, which dates back to Adam and Eve's original sin. Just as the apostle Peter predicts Jesus' return (1 Peter 1:13), Lamech predicted Jesus' coming (Genesis 5:29).

I drew this conclusion as a result of using biblical cross referencing that took me from Genesis 5:29 to Ruth 4:12. The following details the biblical cross referencing process used in drawing this conclusion. The reader is encouraged to independently check these biblical verses:

Genesis 5:29 — Genesis 3:17-19

Genesis 3:17-19 — Genesis 2:7-8

Genesis 2:7-8 — Genesis 13:10

Genesis 13:10 — Genesis 2:8-10

Genesis 2:8-11 — Genesis 25-18

Genesis 25-18 — Genesis 16:12

Genesis 16:12 — Job 39:5-8

Job 39:5-8 — Job 6:4-5

Job 6:4-5 — Job 16:13-15

Job 16:13-15 — Genesis 37:34

Genesis 37:34 — Genesis 37:29

Genesis 37:29 — Numbers 14:3-6

Numbers 14:3-6 — Numbers 14:31-33

Numbers 14:31-33 — Deuteronomy 2:7

Deuteronomy 2:7 — Deuteronomy 8:1-2

Deuteronomy 8:1-2 — Leviticus 26:3-4

Leviticus 26:3-4 — Leviticus 25:17-19

Leviticus 25:17-19 — Leviticus 25:14-25

Leviticus 25:14-25 — Ruth 4:1-12

In the last biblical cross reference story — Ruth 4:1-12 — Boaz and Ruth are married. Their son, Obed, was the father of Jesse and the grandfather of King David. These individuals were the descendants of Judah and Tamar's son, Pharez, who was the father of Hezron and an ancestor of Jesus Christ.

****

One reason Noah's wife may have been promiscuous was his age. It is noted in Genesis 8:13 that Noah was 601 years old after the flood ended. Most likely, he was beyond the age of procreation. It's written in Genesis 17:17 how Abraham was in shock when God enabled him to father a child at the age of one hundred.

In reference to biblical time, it is recorded that some of the first men in the Bible, e.g., Adam, Seth, Enos, Cainan, Jared, Methuselah, and Noah lived more than 900 years (Genesis 5:1-27 and 9:28). Their life spans may not literally mean a full 900 years as we would describe that length of time today. The LASB in a footnote on page 15 provides the following question and three explanations:

"How did these people live so long? Some believe that the ages listed here were lengths of family dynasties rather than ages of individual men. Those who think these were actual ages offer three explanations: (1) The human race was more genetically pure in this early time period, so there was less disease to shorten life spans; (2) no rain had yet fallen on the earth, and the expanse of water "above" (1:7) kept out harmful cosmic rays and shielded people from environmental factors that hasten aging; (3) God gave people longer lives so they would have time to "fill the earth" (1:28)."

Here's my explanation. Moses was born in 1526 B.C. and wrote the book of Genesis around 1445 B.C. over a thousand years before the introduction of the Roman calendar commonly used in today's society. Moses' concept of time when recording biblical character's ages most likely was different and not based on the lunar or solar calendar.

Chapter 11 – Miscegenation

I believe the following story ties black people into the lineage of Jesus Christ. Most who are familiar with the Bible know the promise God made to Abraham to make a nation out of his son, Isaac's descendants. What is generally not known is the promise God made to Abraham about providing a nation for his illegitimate son, Ishmael's descendants as well. The following story tells how the two branches of Abraham's family integrated. This integration fulfills the promises God made to Abraham when he promised a nation to his son Isaac and one to his illegitimate son, Ishmael.

When Hagar ran away from her master, Sarai, an angel of the Lord found her in the wilderness, "And the angel of the LORD said unto her, I will multiply thy seed [Ishmael] exceedingly, that it shall not be numbered for multitude (Genesis 16:10)."

God later made the same promise to Abraham; "And God said unto Abraham, Let it not be grievous in thy sight because of the lad, and because of thy bondwoman; in all that Sarah hast said unto thee, hearken unto her voice; for in Isaac shall thy seed be called. And also of the son of the bondwoman will I make a nation because he is thy seed (Genesis 21:12-13). I believe the fulfillment of this promise starts in Genesis 38:1-30.

****

After Joseph was sold to slave traders (Genesis 37:27-36), his brother Judah left home and moved to Adullam where he married a Canaanite woman who birthed sons named Er, Onan and Shelah. When Er grew up, Judah arranged his marriage to a Canaanite woman named Tamar. Because Er was evil, the Lord killed him.

The law at that time required the surviving brother of a man who died without children to marry the deceased brother's widow. The first-born son of the resulting marriage would be the deceased brother's heir.

Onan was required to marry Tamar, but felt uncomfortable with the arrangement. Whenever he had intercourse with Tamar, Onan would spill his seed on the ground to avoid impregnating her. The Lord frowned on Onan's behavior and killed him, too. Since Onan was Judah's second son to die while being involved with Tamar, Judah, decided not to take a third chance with the fate of his youngest son, Shelah. Judah instructed Tamar, to go home to her parents, remain a widow and wait for Shelah to come of age. Judah was deceiving Tamar as he had no intention of allowing his son to marry her.

Around this time, Judah's wife died. One day, while Judah and his friend Hirah were in Tamar's hometown supervising the shearing of sheep, Tamar received word that Judah was in town. Upon hearing this news, she realized she had not heard from Judah's son, Shelah, regarding marriage, even though she knew Shelah was now a grown man. She changed out of her mourning clothes and sat by the road to Timnah. When Judah passed by, he thought Tamar, who was unrecognizable, was a prostitute and made a proposition, which she accepted with conditions. Tamar's payment for her prostitution services would be a prized goat from Judah's flock. Since the goat was not readily available, Tamar asked Judah to pledge personal items of identification, which he did.

Judah had sex with Tamar, not knowing she was his daughter-in-law. As a result of the sexual relation, Tamar became pregnant.

When he returned home, Judah instructed his friend, Hirah to take the goat back to Tamar and retrieve the personal items that he had left with her. When Hirah arrived in town, Tamar was nowhere to be found and no one seemed to know her or that she even existed. Hirah took this report back to Judah, who said to let Tamar keep the personal items.

Several months later, Judah received word that his daughter-in-law, Tamar, was pregnant from prostituting and he became outraged. Judah ordered Tamar to be burned. At the last moment, Tamar produced Judah's personal items of identification and said, "The man who owns this identification seal and walking stick is the father of my child. Do you recognize them?" Judah acknowledged the items belonged to him and said Tamar was more right than him. Consequently, he granted Tamar her freedom. Tamar's pregnancy produced twin sons, Pharez and Zarah. Through some strange twist of fate, Zarah was actually to have been the first-born. According to the tradition of the time, when the first-born, Zarah, reached out his hand, the midwife tied a scarlet thread around it.

According to the LASB, you will find in the footnote on

page 71, a note indicating "Judah and Tamar are direct ancestors of Jesus Christ (See Matthew 1:1-6)." What the footnote does not say is that Tamar is Jesus' direct ancestor because she was the mother of Pharez and the grandmother of Hezron.

Pharez was a Canaanite through his mother's blood and a Semite through his father's blood. Pharez, with Canaanite and Semite blood, was a direct descendant of Noah's sons, Ham and Shem and Ham's son, Canaan, who was also Noah's stepson and grandson. From this combination of bloodlines, comes Jesus Christ. Hezron the grandson of Tamar and Judah, like his mother and father, was also a Canaanite and Semite. Hezron ties the genealogy going forward to King David and Solomon to Jesus (1 Chronicles 2:9 – 13, Matthew 1: 3 – 16 and Ruth 4:18- 22).

****

According to Dr. Herbert Lockyer in his book, *All the Women of the Bible,*[31] "Er, the oldest son of Judah — was, like Tamar, also a Canaanite." Dr. Lockyer goes on to say the following about Er's mother, Tamar: "The Bible is silent as to her genealogy. All we know is that she was a Canaanite as her heathen name suggests, and that when widowed the second time, she returned to her father's home, but who he was and where he lived we are not told. What we do know is that when she married into the family of Judah, heartache and tragedy were her lot." I declare what we do know is that Tamar was a descendant of Noah's stepson and grandson, Canaan, whose descendants were cursed by him.

Since Tamar was a Canaanite, Noah's curse on the descendants of Canaan would also affect her family tree. That family tree would include Tamar's grandson, Hezron, also the grandson of Judah — a descendant of Abraham. This is significant as it means Hezron and his descendants were enslaved in Egypt for 400 years. The fulfillment of God's promise to Abraham and Hagar continues when Judah takes his sons Pharez and Zarah to Egypt as part of Jacob's family (Genesis 46:12). Could this be the origin of the family feud between Judah and Israel? There are several biblical scriptures, which reference this feud:

- 1Kings 15:16 – there was a constant war between King Asa of Judah and King Baasha of Israel.

- 1 Chronicles 13:6 – Then David and all Israel went to Baalah of Judah to bring back the Ark of god, which bears the name of the LORD who is enthroned between the cherubim.

- Isaiah 11:13 – Then at last the jealousy between Israel and Judah will end. They will not fight against each other anymore.

- Zechariah 11:14 – Then I broke my other staff, Union, to show that the bond of unity between Judah and Israel was broken.

****

The following biblical cross references may provide information about Tamar's ancestors. These references create a path that lead directly to Genesis 9:25 where Noah curses the descendants of Canaan. According to the curse, the descendants of Canaan will be servants to Shem and Japheth.

The cross references begins with Genesis 38:6 in the LASB. This verse recounts the story of Jacob's son, Judah arranging his son's marriage to Tamar. The same verse cross references Matthew 1:3. When reading this verse in the *New International Version Study Bible* (NIV),[32] we learn that Judah and Tamar had two sons, Pharez and Zarah. Their son, Pharez is the father of Hezron whose family lineage leads to Jesus Christ.

Continuing in the NIV, Matthew 1:3 cross reference Genesis 38:27-30, which clarifies Tamar sons, Pharez and Zarah were twins. From this point, the cross reference leads back to Genesis 25:24-25 in the LASB. We learn of the birth of Isaac and Rebekah's twins, Jacob and Esau. This story focuses on the birth of Esau.

The story reveals how Esau received his name. He was red and had so much hair on his body, his parents thought he was wearing clothing (Genesis 25:25). Esau's story cross references Genesis 27:11-12.

In this story, Jacob was trying to explain to his mother that the trick to fool his father, Isaac, wouldn't work. If his father discovered the trick, he [Jacob] would receive a curse from his father rather than the blessing he was seeking. After learning his father Isaac, bestowed the blessing on Jacob, Esau was full of anger. Esau visited his uncle Ishmael and married one of his daughters (Genesis 28:9) "in addition to the wives he already had." This, too, is significant: Esau's uncle Ishmael was the illegitimate son of Abraham by Hagar, his wife Sarai's Egyptian servant.

Genesis 27:12 cross references Genesis 9:25; the story of Noah cursing his grandson and stepson, Canaan, the son of Ham. "Then he cursed the descendants of Canaan, the son of Ham: "A curse on the Canaanites! May they be the lowest of servants to the descendants of Shem and Japheth." I believe these cross references reveal Tamar's ancestors and descendants, as was noted in the previous chapter, were under Noah's curse on Canaan's descendants.

I now believe, the four "heads" or "branches" first mentioned in Genesis 2:10 (And a river went out of Eden to water the garden; and from thence it was parted, and became into four heads/ branches) refers to the families of Shem, Ham, Japheth and Canaan (Genesis 9:18). The key word in Genesis 2:10 is "head" or its synonym, "branch." Webster's defines branch as "a line of family descent stemming from a particular ancestor, as distinguished from some other line or lines from the same stock; a division of a family."

One can also infer meaning from the reference to "river" that we know is a "r(y)ver" and "watering" the garden which we now know refers to Eve being pregnant. The ancestors Adam and Eve left the Garden of Eden and multiplied, much like a garden might grow or multiply when cared for and watered. The words "from thence it was parted" could refer to the multitude of directions across the world the family descendants of Adam and Eve reached; thereby creating many nations, i.e. the nations God promised Abraham to make out of the descendants of his son Isaac, and his illegitimate son Ishmael.

If we trace back the branches of "water," or ancestral lineage, we see Adam and Eve. In this scenario, the ancestors are Adam and Eve. The family descent is the family of Noah and his sons, Shem, Ham and Japheth. Ham's son, Canaan, also Noah's stepson and grandson, is a fourth head and the most prominently known and recognized family head. Canaan was the father of the wicked Canaanites who were eventually wiped off the face of the earth. Their reason for existing was fulfilled when Tamar, their direct descendant, was impregnated by Judah, the direct descendant of Noah's son, Shem. Tamar and Judah's son, Pharez, merged the families of Shem and Ham. This merger led to the birth of Pharez's son Hezron, a direct ancestor of Jesus Christ. Hundreds of years earlier, God made a covenant with Abram to make him the father of many nations. At the time of the covenant God changed Abram's name to Abra**ham** to reflect what was to come (Genesis 17:5).

In the NIV, the cross reference to Genesis 2:11 (One of these branches is the Pishon, which flows around the entire land of Havilah, where gold is found) is Genesis 10:6-8 (The sons of Ham: Cush … and Canaan. The sons of Cush: … Havilah… Cush was the father of Nimrod) connects the families of Ham's son, Cush and Abraham's illegitimate son, Ishmael. The biblical link that connects the family of Abraham's son, Ishmael, to Ham's son, Cush, to Ham's grandson, Nimrod, shows up in the LASB where

Genesis 2:11 cross references to Genesis 25:18 (Ishmael's descendants were scattered across the country from Havilah to Shur, which is east of Egypt in the direction of Asshur. The clans descended from Ishmael camped close to one another). From this we learn that Ishmael and his descendants settled in Havilah.

The reference to Pishon being the first is of key importance, as it is one of the four r(y)vers branching off from a single r(y)ver within Eden. Again, this is another reference supporting the idea of life in Eden with Adam and Eve, branching off throughout the world like rivers. One could say that beyond the confines of the Garden, the single r(y)ver separates into four branches that may represent Noah's family — Shem, Ham, Japheth and Canaan.

In other words, the r(y)ver of Eden provides nourishment to the rest of the world with its life-giving waters, i.e., the birth of many nations, seen through God's promise to Abraham to provide nations out of the descendants of his son Isaac and his illegitimate son Ishmael. In the NIV, the cross reference Havilah first appears is Genesis 2:11. The verse reads; "The name of the first is the Pishon; it winds through the entire land of Havilah, where there is gold." Genesis 2:11 cross references to Genesis 10:6-8, which I believe connects Ishmael to Cush, who was the grandson of Noah and the son of Ham. This makes Tamar, the Canaanite, a descendant of Ham's son, Canaan. The key word in Genesis 2:11 is "first." According to Webster's it is defined as "being before all others with respect to time, order, rank, importance, etc., used as the ordinal number of one." I believe the word "first" is referring to the first "river" or "r(y)ver," meaning Ishmael, the first son of Abraham, whose descendants settled the land of Havilah.

Chapter 12 – From Canaan to Egypt

There is a well-known Bible story where Jacob's sons sold their brother, Joseph, to slave traders. After being sold into slavery, Joseph ended up in Egypt. While in Egypt he gained favor with the Pharaoh and eventually held a high leadership position. One day, Joseph asked the Pharaoh if he could bring his family from Canaan to Egypt to live with him. At the time, the people in Canaan were experiencing a deadly famine. The Pharaoh agreed. Ironically, Joseph commissioned his brothers, who once sold him to slave traders, to travel to Canaan and bring the entire family to Egypt. Joseph's family consisted of his wife, who was a native Egyptian, and their two sons, born while he was in Egypt, and his father, Jacob, and all Jacob's descendants (Genesis 46:6-27). There is no mention of Tamar, the mother who was unknowingly impregnated by Jacob's son, Judah. Tamar's pregnancy produced sons, Pharez and Zarah who were included among Jacob's relocated descendants (Genesis 46:12).

Imagine the scene, Joseph's brothers coming back to Canaan to pick up and transport their father's family. The brothers arrived in the Pharaoh's wagons. Word spreads around Canaan, Pharaoh has extended a special invitation to Jacob's family to come to Egypt, where they would "live off the fat of the land" (Genesis 45:18). The Pharaoh had assigned the best territory in Egypt to Jacob's family upon their return. Remember, there was a famine in Canaan and Jacob's family was leaving behind starving

Canaanites. Tamar, the mother of Judah's sons, Pharez and Zarah was included among those left behind. This would have made for a lot of bitterness and envy. It is possible a story like this would remain in Canaanite folklore for generations.

I believe Noah's curse on the descendants of Canaan continued to be fulfilled when Jacob moved his entire family to Egypt, including Pharez (Genesis 46:28-34). Through his mother, Tamar, Pharez was a descendant of the cursed Canaanites. According to Dr. Herbert Lockyer in All the Women of the Bible, "through Pharez, Judah and Tamar became ancestors of Jesus Christ (Matthew 1:3)." Pharez's son, Hezron would be born in Egypt (Gen 46:12) and the lineage of Jesus Christ would come from Hezron's family tree as noted in Matthews 1:3-17 and Ruth 4:18-22. Over the next 400 years, Hezron's descendants became slaves of subsequent Pharaohs. During this period, the family grew to number two million souls (Exodus 12:37).

****

On Tuesday evening, October 17, 2006, I found a critical missing link. I had been searching biblically for a way to tie Tamar, the Canaanite, to Adam and Eve and to Noah and his son, Ham. According to Genesis 10:6-12 and 1 Chronicles 1:8-10, Canaan was the fourth son of Ham and an uncle of Nimrod. The link to Tamar, the Canaanite, is through Ham's son, Canaan, who was the father of the Canaanites.

The Tamar mystery reveals itself in Genesis 2:25, which take the reader back to the story of Adam and Eve. It reads,

"Now, although Adam and his wife were both naked, neither of them felt any shame." This verse cross references Genesis 10:11-12, the story of Ham's grandson, Nimrod who extends "his reign to Assyria, where he built Nineveh." This verse cross referenced the book of Micah 5:2-6. It reads, "But you, O Bethlehem Ephrathah, are only a small village in Judah. Yet a ruler of Israel will come from you, one whose origins are from the distant past."

This made me stop and consider whether the previous verse refers to Jesus' ancestors as being Adam, Eve and Nimrod. Their origins are from the distant past. The verse continues reading, "The people of Israel will be abandoned to their enemies until the time when the woman in labor gives birth to her son." This verse appears to refer to Mary giving birth to Jesus. The verse continues reading, "When the Assyrians invade our land and break through our defenses, we will appoint seven rulers to watch over us, eight princes to lead us. They will rule Assyria with drawn swords and enter the gates of the land of Nimrod [the Babylonian Empire]." The verses, Micah 5:2-6 cross reference back to previously mentioned Genesis 10:8-12. These verses converse about Nimrod, the grandson of Ham and son of Cush. Nimrod became a heroic warrior and mighty hunter in the Lord's sight.

"His name became proverbial, and people would speak of someone as being "like Nimrod, a mighty hunter in the Lord's sight. He built the foundation for his empire in the land of Babylonia, with the cities of Babel, Erech, Akkad, and Calneh. From there he extended his reign to Assyria, where he built Nineveh, Rehoboth-ir, Calah, and Resen — the main city of the empire, located between Nineveh and Calah."

The preceding cross references tie Tamar, the Canaanite, to Adam and Eve, Noah and his son, Ham who is Nimrod's grandfather.

As I was writing the manuscript, the constantly lingering question; "How did the children of Israel end up in the United States of America?" I knew without suggesting this answer, there would be a gigantic hole in the story, which would leave the story void of credibility.

Chapter 13 - From Canaan to America

What has turned out to be the last chapter in the book was actually one of the first written. In the early stage of writing Entering the Promised Land, the first part of this chapter served as an inspiration to continue the time-consuming and tedious research required to write this book.

One Saturday morning in May 2006, my wife left a copy of a Houston Chronicle newspaper article on my desk. The article detailed how the Houston Independent School District had received a corporate donation of an Africana encyclopedia from a major investment bank.

Later that morning, while working in my office, I took time to read the article. It sparked my interest enough to go to the bookstore and purchase the book. The customer service representative thought the last book had been sold. After a lengthy computer search, the representative informed me there was one book in stock. When we went to the African-American book section to retrieve it, I decided to see what other books on black history might be of interest. The first book I picked up from the shelf was titled, *History of Slavery,*[33] written by Susanne Everett. I read the book's introduction and was amazed to learn how the children of Israel may have traveled from the Middle East to the west coast of Africa.

Earlier, in an opinion piece which ran in the Houston Chronicle's May 5, 2006 issue,[34] the Washington Post's nationally syndicated columnist Charles Krauthammer wrote that the 135 A.D. Jewish Revolt against the Roman army was so brutal that the surviving Jews scattered and were not heard from again for more than 1,800 years. The logical question is what happened to the Jews during this long period of time? After the 135 A.D. Jewish Revolt, history records that the Semite children of Israel, descendants of Noah's son, Shem, fled to Europe and were not heard from again as a Hebrew-speaking people until the 1880s. Meanwhile, history is silent on Ham's descendants. In fact, it appears historians have either deleted or ignored their history entirely. I believe the descendants of Noah's son, Ham, also fled during this uprising from Judea into the sub-Sahara regions of Africa.

In the *History of Slavery's* introduction, Professor Roger Anstey says; "Quite unambiguously [clearly], however, was the slavery which existed in parts of the Mediterranean basin in the Middle [Dark] Ages and which was principally fed by the Islamic merchants' trade route across the Sahara from the interior of West Africa."

Webster's New World College Dictionary[35] defines the Middle Ages as the period of European history between ancient and modern times, A.D. 476 to 1450. This is also the period when there is no recorded history of the modern-day Jew. This is also the period when there is no recorded history of the black children of Israel, who I believe were direct descendants of Noah's son, Ham. According to the Webster's definition of the "Dark Ages the Middle Ages" — "this period in Europe was characterized by intellectual stagnation, widespread ignorance and poverty, and cultural decline." This is also the period when the Hebrew language was considered dead. One might ask if Europe's intellectual stagnation was a result of millions of Jews being displaced and their subsequent inability to contribute to society's intellectual growth.

Once Ham's descendants arrived in sub-Saharan Africa, they may have faced the prospect of enslavement. Professor Anstey continues; "Although the slaves traversing this desert route probably never numbered more than 10,000 a year, and may usually have been many less, such a figure indicates the significance of the institution of medieval slavery."

Professor Anstey goes on to say; "The compromise of the Medieval Church was in effect to accept the institution [of slavery] but to urge good treatment of slaves and, on occasion, the liberation of captives, especially those of one's own skin color." An example of a white slave owned by whites would be Spartacus. Professor Anstey goes on to say that "the Ancient World mostly accepted slavery. Although there were exceptions, such as the Stoics, the essential text was Aristotle's: 'From the hour of their birth, some are marked out for subjection, others for rule.'" The Stoics' philosophy, founded by Zeno, taught that men should be free from passion, unmoved by joy or grief, and submit without complaint to unavoidable necessity.

According to The New Encyclopaedia Britannica, Aristotle was an "organizer of research." "He surveyed the whole field of human knowledge as it was known in the Mediterranean world in his day: and his writings long influenced Western and Muslim thought." It appears Aristotle's thoughts of men being marked for subjection and rule profoundly impacted the thinking of slavery.

****

The biblical story of Joseph in Genesis 37 may offer insight into the fate of some of Ham's descendants after their arrival in sub-Saharan Africa. Joseph's story details how his brothers sold him to slave traders. As Jacob's favorite son, Joseph gave reports to his father whenever his brothers misbehaved. Joseph would also recount to his brothers and father dreams in which his brothers and father would one day bow down to him.

In recounting these dreams to his brothers, Joseph created a love-hate relationship between himself and his brothers. One day, Joseph's brothers were out tending the sheep and were running late. Joseph's father noticed the boys were late returning home and instructed Joseph to go and check on them. When Joseph caught up with his brothers, they saw him in the distance before he saw them. So jealous were they of their younger brother that they plotted to kill him.

One of the brothers, Reuben, suggested leaving Joseph in a dried-up water pit to die, as opposed to killing him immediately. Reuben planned to return to the pit later and secretly take Joseph back to their father. After leaving his brothers with Joseph and later returning, he discovered Joseph was gone. Unbeknown to Reuben, his brother Judah convinced the others to sell Joseph to slave traders for 20 pieces of silver rather than kill him. The transaction was completed and Joseph ended up in Egypt.

When Reuben returned and discovered that Joseph was not in the pit, he reported to his brothers that Joseph was missing. The brothers feigned shock and together they hatched a scheme to convince their father that a wild animal had killed Joseph. They dipped Joseph's beautiful robe in the blood of a goat they had killed and later showed the robe to their father, who recognized it immediately. Upon seeing the blood soaked robe, Jacob mourned the death of his favorite son, Joseph.

As this story reveals, the slave trade dates back more than fifteen hundred years before the birth of Jesus Christ. I believe that after the 135 A.D. Jewish Revolt, the descendants of Ham, the black Jews, just like their Semite brothers, were killed, persecuted or forced into a nomadic life leaving them vulnerable to slave traders.

****

Biblical history tells the story of Shem's descendants, the modern-day Jews, scattering to Germany and Russia. German Jews emigrated to the United States in the first half of the 19th century and Russian Jews emigrated to the United States in the last decade of that century and the early 1900's. So the question remains: How did Ham's descendants, the modern-day African-Americans, end up in the United States as slaves?

Although there is no recorded history of the black children of Israel, I believe Ham's descendants scattered to Ethiopia, Egypt and other nearby parts of Africa. It's only natural for one to flee where one can blend with the locals. Or so they thought! While they blended in terms of skin color, everyone knows when the new kid comes to town.

It's conceivable that the black children of Israel were not

welcomed. In fact, it's conceivable that the locals turned the children over to the descendants of the same slave traders who bought Joseph. The slave traders captured the children of Israel and conducted business as usual. They took them on caravans across the Sahara Desert to the west coast of Africa where they were sold. From there, the children ended up on slave ships headed to the United States of America.

As slaves on the plantations in the South, the white slave masters were surprised how the slaves readily adopted Christianity. In the introduction of Susanne Everett's book, History of Slavery, Professor Roger Anstey writes, "Interestingly, one dimension of a paradoxical relationship between slave and master in the Southern states, as Professor Genovese emphasizes in *Roll, Jordan, Roll,* was that the slave appropriated the white man's mainly Evangelistical Christianity."

Maybe the slaves adopted the white man's religion because the Old Testament Bible and the indwelling of the Holy Spirit was the basis of their religion. The slave's religion may not have been called by the English word, "Christianity," but the foundation of their beliefs was the same as that of the slave master's religion. If these American slaves were the descendants of the children of Israel who were once held captive by the Romans, Judaism, the root of this white man's religion, would have had been handed down through the generations dating back before the birth of Jesus Christ.

During times of persecution or other hardships, the one thing a spiritual person holds on to for survival is their faith. One does not need a church or a Bible to have faith in God. A person's faith can be maintained through prayer while on the run or while held in captivity.

****

Whether or not one agrees with my assertions about the history of black people, the Bible makes one lesson very clear: In order to enter the Promised Land, if black people are to achieve economic parity in the U.S.A., black people must take the lessons from the Bible and *live them with a knowing faith*.

A May 2007 weekend reunion with college fraternity brothers helped reveal the most crucial point I have been trying to make in writing *Entering the Promise Land*. It dawned on me that the Civil Rights Movement as defined by Dr. King's work was never finished. As many of his speeches prove, Dr. King repeatedly placed a special emphasis on black people needing to push much harder for economic equality along with social equality. This approach lost its intensity after his death.

Fortunately, before his death, Dr. King took time from his hectic schedule to write the book, *Where Do We Go from Here: Chaos or Community?* According to its introduction in the book, *A Testament of Hope – The Essential Writings and Speeches of Martin Luther King, Jr.,* Dr. King traveled to Jamaica to finish writing the book. His schedule was grueling as "he worked twenty-hour days, traveled approximately 325,000 miles per year, and often gave as many as 450 speeches per year." I describe his book as a message from the grave. When he gave his final speech, I See the Promised Land, at "[the Bishop Charles] Mason Temple in Memphis, Tennessee" on April 3, 1968, it was a summary of this book with the exception of the quote, which most are familiar with, "I've been to the mountaintop ... I've seen the promised land." As previously mentioned, since Dr. King's death, I believe the Civil Rights Movement never ended. One could easily say the movement has been on pause for 40 years. Remember, his prophecy, "we as a [black] people will get to the promised land," has not been fulfilled.

I believe, the answers to black people entering the Promised Land, participating in the economic prosperity of the U.S.A., lies in taking appropriate actions according to Dr. King's instructions as outlined in his last speech. In the speech, Dr. King addressed the following issues:

- Unity – Dr. King encouraged black people to work together to solve economic issues. He likened the Pharaoh as the equivalent of today's U.S. white establishment. Specifically, he explained how those in power can find ways to keep an oppressed people divided amongst themselves. The Pharaoh, during the enslavement of the children of Israel, took straws away from the slaves making bricks, which made their task harder and resulted in them complaining to their leader, Moses, thus dividing the people (Exodus 5:6-23). To paraphrase the motto of the United States of America; united black people stand, divided black people fall.

- Spiritualism – Dr. King noted in his last speech that while we want to talk about long white robes over yonder, but the reality is that God's children need food and clothing right here and now. It's okay to prepare for the hereafter. But while on earth, black people need to focus on earthly matters such as food, clothing and shelter.

- Pressuring ministers – Dr. King said, "Somehow the preacher must be an Amos, and say, 'let justice roll down like waters and righteousness like a mighty stream.'" I believe Dr. King was trying to admonish ministers to remember that, as leaders, they have a responsibility to play a significant leadership role and demand better living standards for the people they have been entrusted to lead. Indeed, Dr. King went on to say, "Somehow, the preacher must say with Jesus, 'The spirit of the Lord is upon me, because he hath anointed me to deal with the problems of the poor.'" Dr. King criticized some black ministers for their motives. In his book, *"Where Do We Go From Here,"* he writes that some black preachers are "more concerned about the size of the wheel base on their automobiles than about the quality of their service to the community."

- Strengthening black institutions – Dr. King instructed black people to conduct business with each other. Whenever a black dollar is spent, every effort should be made to spend it with a black business. Unfortunately, in the year 2007, Dr. King's message remains ignored as evidenced by the continued impoverished state of the black business community.

- Boycotting companies that abuse their relationship with

black people – Dr. King encouraged the people to make demands on businesses where black people spend their money. Demand reciprocal relationships with corporate America and other businesses that conduct trade with black people. If black people spend money with any non-black business, those businesses in return should be expected to spend some of their money with the black community. Corporate dollars spent in the black community should help provide jobs with opportunities for career growth and a path to reach the top; provide significant contracts with black businesses; and, provide charitable contributions to black not-for-profits.

I can imagine if Dr. King were alive today he would urge black people to set up metrics to verify growth in the areas of hiring, contracting, and charitable contributions. As former President Ronald W. Reagan said, "Trust, but verify."

- Help those who are less fortunate – Dr. King uses the parable of the Levite and the Good Samaritan. The Levite asked if I stop and help this man in trouble, what will happen to me. "The Good Samaritan ... reversed the question: "If I do not stop to help this man, what will happen to him?" (Luke 10:31-35). Dr. King was reminding black people to stop and lend a helping hand to their brothers and sisters who were less fortunate.

Also in the book, *Where Do We Go From Here?*, Dr. King writes, "It is a disappointment with the Negro middle class that has sailed or struggled out of the muddy ponds into the relatively fresh-flowing waters of the mainstream, and in the process has forgotten the stench of the backwaters where their brothers are still drowning."

Remember the rabbi's comments in Chapter 1 regarding the wealthy and poor Jews who came to America from Germany and Russia in the 1880s and early 1900s, respectively. It was the classic case of the rich snubbing the poor, until the rich Jews realized they could not truly elevate themselves unless they helped empower their poor brethren.

The message that Dr. King and the rabbi are both trying to drive home is repeatedly found in the Bible itself. The message is those who feel they are secure in their current economic status should never assume they are beyond the misery afflicting their poor brothers and sisters. To paraquotation Genesis 31:42 or Romans 12:3, "but for the grace of God go I."

- Death – In Dr. King's final recorded speech on April 3, 1968, he said, "I just want to do God's will. And He's allowed me to go up to the mountain. And I've looked over. And I've seen the promised land." Notice that Dr. King said he has *seen* the Promised Land. There is emphasis on the word "seen," which is the past participle of "see," which means to "perceive with the eyes." In the context of his 1963 speech, "I Have a Dream," the word "dream" is employed to mean "a succession of images, thoughts, or emotions passing through the mind during sleep." But by 1968, it seems, Dr. King emphasized what he had *seen* to make clear he was no longer simply *dreaming* about progress. Also, in his final speech, Dr. King said death caused him no fear — perhaps to remind us that there is no place for fear when you are fighting for your beliefs and your survival.

Again, in the book, *Where Do We Go From Here?*, Dr. King writes about the training of a black slave as written by historian Kenneth Stampp. The slave training was documented in manuals produced by the slaveowners. It focused on "the psychological indoctrination that was necessary from the master's viewpoint to make a good slave." The five areas of training:

1.   Maintain strict discipline
2.   Implant a consciousness of personal inferiority
3.   Implant a sense of the master's enormous power
4.   The slave must take an interest in the master's enterprise and accept a standard of good conduct.
5.   Impress Negroes with their helplessness; to create in them a habit of perfect dependence upon their masters.

In summation Dr. King writes, "Here, then, was the way to produce a perfect slave. Accustom him to rigid discipline, demand from him unconditional submission, impress upon him a sense of his innate inferiority, develop in him a paralyzing fear of white men, train him to adopt the master's code of good behavior, and instill in him a sense of complete dependence." What Dr. King omits is how "paralyzing fear" was instilled with brutality and inhumane treatment to break a human being who does not conform. Imagine the chilling message that the torture of a man or woman sent to the family and to other slaves.

Never forget that black people's ancestors endured 244 years of this treatment during slavery and brutality such as lynching during the Jim Crow era until 1959. And, let us not forget that as recently as June 16, 2000, television news and newspapers across the country reported the lynching of Raynard Johnson, a 17 year old who lived in Kokomo, Mississippi. The lynching of Johnson reminded many of the 1955 lynching of Emmett Till who supposedly whistled at a white woman.

During the period of slavery and Jim Crow, each subsequent generation endured what some would describe as inhumane physical and psychological treatment. The effects of training the slave and ongoing mental abuse afterward, may still linger in some black people to this day. The following illustrates 244 years or 12 generations of slavery in today's black family with an American heritage:

1. Parents were slaves
2. Grand parents were slaves
3. Great-grand parents were slaves
4. Great-great- grand parents were slaves
5. Great-great-great grand parents were slaves

6. Great-great-great-great grand parents were slaves

7. Great-great-great-great-great grand parents were slaves

8. Great-great-great-great-great-great grand parents were slaves

9. Great-great-great-great-great-great-great grand parents were slaves

10. Great-great-great- great-great-great-great-great grand parents were slaves

11. Great-great-great- great-great-great-great-great-great grand parents were slaves

12. Great-great-great- great-great-great-great-great-great-great grand parents were slaves

Hopefully, this illustration will allow you to understand the magnitude of slavery on a black person's family and how its effects may still impact the thinking of a black person, even today. Keep in mind, this illustration does not take into account the 100 years of Jim Crow laws that could be described as semi-slavery. The Jim Crow era severely limited opportunities for advancement and growth among blacks. I don't think it takes a psychiatrist to figure out that after the signing of the Civil Rights Act in 1964, some people have yet to realize that it takes more than written laws to erase centuries of brainwashing and instilled hatred. Maybe, this is why Dr. King wrote about this subject in his book, *Where Do We Go From Here?* He wrote:

> *"For years the Negro has been taught that*
> *he is nobody, that his color is a sign of his bio-*

logical depravity, that his being has been stamped with an indelible imprint of inferiority, that his whole history has been soiled with the filth of worthlessness. All too few people realized how slavery and racial segregation have scarred the soul and wounded the spirit of the black man. The whole dirty business of slavery was based on the premise that the Negro was a thing to be used, not a person to be respected."

Time is running out and the "wilderness" ordeal is drawing to a conclusion. Black people living in America have struggled mightily while living in or near poverty for almost 400 years. It is imperative that the black community develop and implement a strategic plan before the last black generation that survived the Jim Crow era passes away. The time is now.

As Dr. King so eloquently stated, "The Negro will only be truly free when he reaches down to the inner depths of his own being and signs with the pen and ink of assertive selfhood his own emancipation proclamation. With a spirit straining toward self-abnegation and say to himself and the world: 'I am somebody. I am a person. I am a man with dignity and honor. I have a rich and noble history, however painful and exploited that history has been. I am black and comely.' This self-affirmation is the black man's need made compelling by the white man's crimes against him. This is positive and necessary power for black people."

Always remember, black people are mentally and physically strong and have a rich and proud history. You should not be ashamed of being the descendant of slaves; those who enslaved should have borne that shame. As Dr. McCalep wrote in his book, *When Black Men Stretch Their Hands to God*: "Slavery is due to the sin of the slaveholder and not the slave."

Although deleted from written history, black people are descendants of the children of Israel. Our ancestors survived captivity in Egypt, Babylonia, Assyria, the Roman Empire, caravans across the Sahara Desert, slave ships to America in deplorable conditions, brutal life on the plantation, and 100 years of Jim Crow. As a people, if that didn't wipe us off the face of the earth, nothing can or will other than God, Himself. As the Lord promised Abraham, "As for Ishmael, I will bless him also, just as you have asked. I will cause him to multiply and become a great nation (Genesis 17:20).

Today, black people must work daily to break what remains of the imposed generational mental shackles. Once the shackles have been broken, the movement will arise once again — driven by people with uncompromised principles. If black people adhere, Dr. King's prophecy will be fulfilled and black people will enter the Promised Land.

Many years ago my high school literature teacher first introduced the poem, *"Invictus"*[36] by William Ernest Henley, to my classmates and me. There were other poems, but "Invictus" was special. Reciting poetry to the students was my teacher's way of breathing life into learning. It was not until many years later, I realized the poem "Invictus" was not only educational but also appropriate for a struggling black people in 1966 and, in my opinion, remains so today. I pray that it may be helpful on your journey. I share it with you for that reason.

Invictus

Out of the night that covers me,
Black as the Pit from pole to pole,
I thank whatever gods may be
For my unconquerable soul.

In the fell clutch of circumstance
I have not winced nor cried aloud.
Under the bludgeonings of chance
My head is bloody, but unbowed.

Beyond this place of wrath and tears
Looms but the Horror of the shade,
And yet the menace of the years
Finds, and shall find me, unafraid.

It matters not how strait the gate,
How charged with punishments the scroll,
I am the master of my fate:
I am the captain of my soul.

Through study and revelation, my life has changed in a very short time. Where there was once anger and frustration, there now is excitement and acceptance. Why? Because I know that black people *can* enter the Promised Land. We can do it for ourselves as a people, as a family, by understanding our biblical history and taking control of our own destiny. Black people cannot rely on anyone other than God and themselves when striving to solve economic and social problems. That is one lesson I learned from my December 2002 speech to the Greater Houston Partnership and trying to survive daily as an African-American businessman.

Black people must learn what Jewish immigrants knew when they came to America in the 1880s, what many Latin American immigrants know as they risk their lives crossing the US-Mexican border; and what many other ethnic groups know who go through the standard immigration process. The United States of America is the Promised Land.

At the end of the day, we need to take control of our own destinies. Yes, life has dealt some of us what a gambler would describe as a bad hand. We need to understand that nothing will change in our lives unless we make it change. We cannot wait for Jesus Christ or anyone else to come and put things right for us. While here on earth, there are steps we can take ourselves to make life better. The black community has been impoverished for nearly 400 years. Fortunately, it won't take another 400 years to get out of poverty. The first step is for strategic minds to develop and implement a plan for the black community based on the principles as outlined by Dr. Martin Luther King, Jr. Consider this a nation-building effort. Think in terms of a plan to cover two generations or 40 years.

My research and my resulting opinions merely scratch the surface on the role played by black people in the Bible and throughout history. Throughout my journey, I have sought the truth.

Indeed, it has been a personal learning journey that was made on the force of my faith, intellect, and a search for redemption in the form of an identified heritage.

I encourage others to investigate for themselves. I am moved to recall the words of Henry Wadsworth Longfellow, from his poem, "A Psalm of Life,"[37] which I learned as a high school student. Obviously, Longfellow was not black, but I believe the following passage fits a people struggling to emerge from a harsh past:

Trust no Future, howe'er pleasant! Let the dead Past bury its dead! Act — act in the living Present! Heart within, and God o'erhead!

Start your own journey — the first step is to read and understand Dr. King's very last message, *I See the Promised Land.* The second step, read his book, *Where Do We Go From Here: Chaos or Community?* Armed with knowledge, our destiny is in our hands. The third and final step is to take control of your life. Who knows exactly how, but we will reach the mountaintop together.

Epilogue

In going back and trying to discover my roots I was led to the importance of fidelity within a family. Without fidelity within a family — being married before you have sex and have children — our moral compass is askew. As a consequence, one can wander in the deserts of this world for a lifetime and never find a way to enter the Promised Land.

Fidelity within a family is a precondition to putting God first and living a purposeful, Godly life. It is difficult to see how God can be first in a person's life without fidelity within the family. We have to go back to the beginning where it all starts with Adam and Eve and their covenant. The Bible tells us that when we are unfaithful to God it begins with being unfaithful to ourselves and to one another. Time and again this example is put before us. As I contemplated more about family and relationships, I had to go back to the first one with Adam and Eve.

To understand and comprehend Adam and Eve's story and its real relevance today, the Bible tells us about other stories of man's fall from grace with God — a fall that continually replays on life's stage like the rerun of an old movie. I believe, what is not well understood and its relevance today to young people and especially to young African- Americans is what actually caused Adam and Eve's fall.

God reminds us of Adam and Eve's fall and what happened in their relationship to cause their fall in other biblical stories: 1)

Noah son's, Ham's infidelity with his stepmother who was also Noah's wife 2) Abraham and his relationship with his wife's servant, Hagar, that produced an illegitimate son named Ishmael 3) Judah impregnating his daughter-in-law, Tamar, which created the all time family feud 4) Samson and Delilah 5) King David taking Bathsheba and having her husband murdered and 6) the many wives and concubines of King Solomon. I believe, these stories are written to remind us how infidelity wrecked Adam and Eve's relationship with God, themselves, and their children and how, even today, it's the number one destroyer of marriages and families.

Remember in the Prologue, I asked scholars maintaining or defending certain dogma about the Bible to re-examine old assumptions. In going back to Adam and Eve and their family relationship, it is my belief that the fullness of biblical scripture related to them and the beginning of mankind on earth has not been completely understood. As a consequence, the richness and the relevance of this scriptural guidance is not fully conveyed or understood by married and unmarried couples, especially vulnerable young black couples.

I believe a more complete understanding of Adam and Eve and their family relationship is crucial to understanding the scripture with regards to fidelity within a family and may be what is needed for the survival of a young couple who desire to live their lives and raise their family in a Godly way. It is my belief that an accurate interpretation of the scripture would provide a spiritual roadmap to help in the understanding of marriage vows, which would keep the family together, "for better or worse," and provide a sound footing for the readers who seek to enter the Promised Land. For this reason, I have included my interpretations of the "Creation of Man"

****

In the "Moment of Discovery" chapter, I asked whether Adam and Eve actually ate "fruit?" Did Eve speak to a "serpent" or were the "fruit" and "serpent" metaphors representative of something else? If not an apple, what was the forbidden fruit? Who was the serpent? After eating the forbidden fruit, why were Adam and Eve banished from the Garden of Eden? What did banishment mean? These questions are but a few that came to mind. I hope the reader will understand the spirit in which I offer my interpretations. They are shared with the intention of encouraging you to read the Scriptures from a different point of view.

Here are my interpretations: First, the prophet Moses wrote the book of Genesis using the customary writing style of his time. Ancient writers had to be vividly descriptive so the reader, who may not have been fortunate to have been schooled or well traveled could form a mental picture of the story based upon the writers detailed and intense description of the place and people surrounding him in those times. Writers had to turn words into pictures in order to make the reader understand clearly what someone or something looked like or how they did something. Invariably, a story written today would be metaphoric to an ancient reader and difficult to understand. Today, the preferred style uses simple, concise language to describe a situation. Today's style would probably seem inadequate to an ancient reader.

****

In the beginning God created Adam and Eve whose primary purpose was to start a family or procreate: "for the Lord God had not caused it to rain upon the earth" (Genesis 2:5). To comprehend this verse, today's reader must understand the metaphoric meaning of the key word "rain" and its relationship to procreation. A synonym for the word "rain" is "shower²," a person or thing that shows, which can be defined as the onset of labor.

From ancient times through today, sex education has always been a very difficult topic to discuss. As a young man growing up in Alabama, the word "rain" was at times associated with sexual intercourse. An adult would counsel, "When it rains, do not forget to wear your raincoat," or "if it's raining, remember to wear protection." In short, sex is the one subject matter where adults use symbolism to avoid graphic language with their children.

The first phrase of Genesis 2:5 reads: "and every plant of the field before it was in the earth, and every herb of the field before it grew." Webster's define a "plant" as a young person and an "herb" as a flowering or developing child.

In Volume VII, page 153 of the OED, Gerarde Herbal makes reference to a child as an "herb" in a 1597 quotation that reads: "Those flowers..that come after growe higher, as children seeking to..ouertop their parents..for which cause it hath been called Herba Impia, that is, the Wicked herbe, of *Herbe Impious."

Translation: Those flowers that bloom later and grow taller are similar to children who attempt to... surpass or rise above their parents ....for this reason it has been called Herba Impia, that is, the "wicked plant," or "impious plant."

I believe Genesis 2:5 is referring to the beginning of man's presence on earth when there were no children because men and women had not begun to procreate. As Genesis 2:5 continues, "...there was not a man to till the ground." In the OED, there is an obsolete definition of the word "till," which means "to seduce." Webster's define seduce as to "persuade or induce to have sexual intercourse."

While discussing my interpretation of "tilling the ground" with my brother, Edward Charles, he thought the Bible's book of Judges 14:18 would provide additional insight into the meaning of the word "till." In this Bible verse, Samson said to the men, "If you hadn't plowed [tilled] with [or seduced] my heifer, you wouldn't have found the answer to my riddle!"

Samson was referring to a riddle he had asked 30 men in his wedding ceremony to solve. The baffled men could not solve the riddle and persuaded his wife to get the answer from Samson. Samson's wife sweet talked him out of the answer and gave it to the men who in turn solved Samson's riddle. Samson became furious, left his wife and returned home. After Samson left, his wife was given in marriage to his best man. This convinced an already suspicious Samson that his wife had been unfaithful to him earlier. Someone, metaphorically, had "plowed" with his "heifer" or literally been involved with his wife sexually.

Samson's metaphor of plowing with his heifer leads me to think of "tilling the ground" in an entirely different way. In defining the word "ground," Webster's uses the phrase, "break ground," which means to take preparatory measures for any undertaking. I now believe the "ground" as mentioned in Genesis 2:5, "there was not a man to till the ground" is a metaphor for men and women who had not been created by God, thus no procreation could occur. I contend the word "ground," like a woman's womb, has the same meaning as where a seed is planted, nurtured, grown and produced.

One of the OED's many definitions of the word, "ground," describes it as "the divine essence or centre of the individual soul, in which mystic union lies." An examination of the key words, "mystic and union," I believe are revealing. "Mystic" is defined as "a person who claims to attain, or believes in the possibility of attaining, insight into mysteries transcending ordinary human knowledge." And, "union" refers to an "act of being united in marriage or sexual intercourse."

****

Adam as the first man on earth, being uncivilized, would receive from God the first rule for orderly societal living, which would be marriage and procreation. The following story examines sex and the role it plays in our lives: Before Adam and Eve started a family, God required them to be married. This requirement is still valid today. God gave these uncivilized individuals basic instructions that were essential to starting a family: Couples must start families only after marriage. The foundation of procreation, then and now, is based on the sacred institution of marriage.

Marriage is the institution from which children are created, nurtured and grown. A solid marriage will ensure children will have an opportunity to grow to adulthood in a proper way. When the children are grown, they too should be married before starting their families.

Although Adam and Eve, the first humans on earth, fit the definition of "barbarians," they were probably much like the newly weds of today — happy, with no secrets and nothing to hide from God or each other. According to Genesis 2:24, the husband and wife are to cleave to each other allowing no other person to come between them. God's instructions for a married couple have not changed to this day.

The married Adam and Eve lived in the Garden of Eden. This "Garden" is described as a "fertile and delightful spot or region" or a "state of mind where there's perfect happiness or bliss." In other words, everything is right with God.

Since there was not yet a social structure, i.e., no minister, no justice of the peace and therefore no formal ceremony, Genesis 2:21 described Adam and Eve's marriage ceremony as a "deep sleep." When reviewing the definitions of the words, "deep" and "sleep," we learn that "deep" refers to heartfelt affections and inextricably involved and "sleep" to engage in sexual intercourse.

There is also strong indication that until the time of the Great Flood and beyond, sexual intercourse was the standard marriage ceremony for men and women. Genesis 6:1-4 reads, "When the human population began to grow rapidly on the earth, the sons of God saw the beautiful women of the human race and took any they wanted as their wives." The key words mentioned are "saw" and "took." As revealed in the chapter, "Noah Curses Canaan," one of the meanings of the word "saw" is "to know," which means "to have sexual intercourse." The word "took" is the past tense of the word "take," which has a sexual connotation that means "to take someone in marriage, to have sexual intercourse with or to possess sexually." This suggests God was not pleased with the crude way men were treating women. In fact, I am sadly reminded of a cave man walking with a club in one hand and dragging a woman by the hair with the other.

Another example of a marriage being consummated by sexual intercourse appears in Genesis 16:3, which reads; "And Sarai Abram's wife took Hagar her maid the Egyptian, after Abram had dwelt ten years in the land of Canaan, and gave her to her husband Abram to be his wife." The key word in the preceding verse "gave," is the past tense of the word "give," which means to offer or yield oneself for sexual intercourse. It appears Sarai gave permission to Abram to have a sexual relationship with Hagar, which consummated their marriage.

Yet another example of a marriage's consummation by sexual intercourse appears in the book of Exodus 2:21-22, which reads; "And Moses was content to dwell with the man and he gave [for sexual intercourse] Moses Zipporah his daughter. And she bare him a son, and he called his name Gershom: for he said, I have been a stranger in a strange land."

One more story of sexual intercourse consummating marriage is that of Ruth and Boaz. Ruth 4:13 reads; "So Boaz took [had sexual intercourse with] Ruth into his home, and she became his wife. When he slept with her, the Lord enabled her to become pregnant and she gave birth to a son."

And finally, when God confronted Adam in the Garden of Eden, Adam reminded God that he "gave" [for sexual intercourse] Eve as his wife (Genesis 3:12). This verse reads, "And the man said, The woman whom thou gavest to be with, she gave me of the tree, and I did eat." The reader should keep in mind that sexual intercourse was in itself, the original marriage ceremony. Adam appears to be shifting the blame to God and Eve. He blames God for introducing Eve to him and Eve for persuading him to "eat" or engage in inappropriate sexual intercourse.

I reached this conclusion that Adam and Eve engaged in inappropriate sexual intercourse by examining various definitions associated with the word "eat." The word "eat" first appeared in a sexual connotation in the late 1920s. Since this slang post-dates the 1611 Holy Bible, its validity in interpreting ancient scripture is questionable.

My hypothesis in trying to find the original definition of the word "eat" led me to search for its synonyms. To have validity, the synonyms must predate the 1611 Holy Bible. What the reader should keep in mind is that as the number of words synonymous with the word "eat" increased, the word "eat" itself may have become less associated with its sexual connotation. People who may have sought to communicate in a more educated or sophisticated manner to describe erotic activity were likely to avoid using simple words like "eat," which are frequently associated with people with a more limited vocabulary.

For example, the first definition of "eat" uses the word "devour" to help define it. The meaning of "devour" on the surface, does not appear to provide insight into Eve engaging in sexual intercourse. However, I believe an examination of other words associated with it does. The definition of "devour" means to swallow or eat up ravenously. The word "ravenous," means "intensely eager for gratification." Webster's defines "gratification" as a source of pleasure. The key word "pleasure" when used as a transitive verb in Webster's New World College Dictionary 4th Edition, means "to give pleasure sexually or to have sexual intercourse."

The definition of "pleasure" as having sexual intercourse leads me to believe Eve wanted someone sexually. I believe the someone she wanted was the "serpent" who was also described in the scripture as a "tree." My research of the words associated with the word "eat" leads me to believe Eve engaged in an extramarital affair with the "serpent" and Adam discovered her infidelity. After being discovered by Adam she convinced him it was okay to engage in extramarital sex.

I have concluded that at the time of Moses' biblical writings, the word "tree" was metaphorically used to describe a man or woman. In Genesis 2:9, it reads, "And out of the ground made the LORD God to grow every tree that is pleasant to the sight, and good for food; the tree of life also in the midst of the garden, and the tree of knowledge of good and evil." I believe as defined by the OED, the word "tree," can be "applied figuratively or **allusively** (metaphorically) to a person."

Since the second chapter of Genesis discusses the creation of man and procreation, I interpret this part of the verse literally as meaning; God created man and woman and was pleased with his creations that were good for producing children. The OED, in one definition equates "food" to "fodder," which is defined as a child or an offspring.

The following is my interpretation of the phrase, "the tree of life also in the midst of the garden, and the tree of knowledge of good and evil."

As in any community, married couples live "in the midst," which means they are "among or are surrounded by" other married couples and people. As in any situation, like Adam and Eve, these married couples and the others living in the area could have succumbed to sin at certain points in their lives. Likewise, the married couples who lived with daily temptations, yet still upheld their marriage vows were metaphorically referred to as the "tree of life."

The "tree of life," also a family tree, represented an Adam and Eve living a sin-free life before they were corrupted by Satan's use of the "serpent" to introduce lust into their relationship. During Adam and Eve's life in the community, God may have given them the following instructions: Maintain a monogamous relationship and your lives together will be happy and prosperous.

On the other hand, the "tree of knowledge of good and evil," represented Adam and Eve after falling prey to temptation by engaging in inappropriate sexual behavior. I believe the "tree of knowledge of good and evil" metaphorically represents a married couple choosing right and/or wrong sexual behavior. My belief that the "tree of knowledge of good and evil" represents both good and bad sexual behavior is bolstered by understanding the meanings of "good" and "evil" and the OED's definition of the word "knowledge." The word "knowledge" archaically means sexual intercourse."

In the KJV Holy Bible, Family Reference Edition, of interest is the title of Genesis, Chapter 3, "The fall of man" found on page three. This chapter tells the story of Adam, Eve and the "serpent." My focus is on the definition of the word "fall," which in Middle English meant "fallen." The definition of "fallen" is defined as a woman who's lost her chastity or sexually active.

****

Since the beginning of time, struggling with extramarital sexual relationships has been mankind's curse. In Genesis 3:1-7, Adam and Eve were confronted with a modern-day problem; a third person tested their marriage relationship through sexual enticement. Eve's sexual transgressions are noted in Genesis 3:6. The verse reads, "And when the woman saw that the tree was good for food, and that it was pleasant to the eyes, and a tree to be desired to make one wise, she took of the fruit thereof, and did eat, and gave also unto her husband with her; and he did eat."

The "serpent," to whom Eve spoke, was Satan and not a snake that crawls on the ground. Even a child would doubt that anyone could talk with a snake. As the central character in this story, the "serpent" as defined by Webster's is "a wily, treacherous, or malicious person." He presented himself as a man and seduced Eve to commit adultery. Eve, on the other hand, viewed Satan as good looking, charming and sexually appealing. Her submission is noted by the definition of the words, "desired — which means "a sexual appetite or a sexual urge" and "took," the past tense of "take"— which means to possess sexually or to have sexual intercourse with."

Later, in the book of Genesis 39:6-20, Joseph, a handsome well built Hebrew slave was often tempted by the wife of a high administrative official who worked for the Pharaoh. This married lady put tremendous pressure on Joseph to sleep with her but he always resisted. One day while working in her house, Joseph found himself confronted by the woman who once again made an unwanted advance. Again, Joseph resisted the temptation. She grabbed Joseph; he pulled away and ran out of the house. While struggling out of the woman's grasp, Joseph's shirt was inadvertently torn.

As the story goes, she cried rape and Joseph was thrown into prison for a crime he did not commit. Unlike Eve, Joseph resisted temptation and was later blessed as opposed to being cursed by God.

In the biblical books, Matthew 16:23, Mark 8:33 and Luke 4:8, Jesus referred to Peter as Satan. Matthew 16:23 reads: "But he turned, and said unto Peter, Get thee behind me, Satan: thou art an offence unto me: for thou savourest not the things that be of God, but those that be of men." Surely, Jesus wasn't saying Peter was actually Satan, but simply using a metaphor to characterize Peter's behavior. This verse reminds me of once hearing the old folks refer to a person misbehaving as having the devil in them. The fruit mentioned in Genesis 2:9, I now believe, was not an "apple" as is commonly portrayed in popular culture. Metaphorically, the "apple or forbidden fruit" literally represented Eve's transgression sexually outside of her marriage. Rather than feeling shame for her sin, Eve persuaded Adam to commit the same sinful act. Their sin of adultery was so egregious, Adam and Eve "died" a spiritual — not physical — death and were forever banished from the "Garden of Eden." The OED defines "die" as theologically to lose spiritual life or suffer spiritual death. And, Webster's define "banish" with its synonym, "ostracize," which implies forced exclusion from society because of disgrace or scandalous behavior.

****

It appears adultery was the original sin and sexual transgression ranked as the first act of disobedience to God, i.e., adultery ranks as the first "root of all evil." The message appears to be marriage is the foundation of a civilized society and the importance of sexual morality and marital fidelity should be instilled in children at an early age. Why not? The status quo has not worked. The Bible's story of the first man finally makes sense. In the beginning God created man and instructed him to procreate. However, before man could procreate, he had to be married. Once married, he could procreate and start a family. After marriage, no other person could be romantically involved with either married partner. If another person defiled the relationship, there would be severe consequences.

The Rhythm and Blues singing group, The O'Jays, in their 1975 hit recording, "Family Reunion," seem to have gotten it correct when they sang that the family is the solution to the world's problems. Although the song was a hit, the message didn't quite get through. If only then and now we adhere to the lyrics of the song and the advice of one of the album's producers, Kenneth Gamble, who said: "Remember the family that prays together stays together." Put the 'unity' back into the family." Achieving and maintaining family unity through prayer and staying together is the hallmark of fidelity within a family and provides the moral compass that is required if one is to enter the Promised Land.

Acknowledgements

For the past five years, I have been writing "Entering the Promised Land." A monumental task made possible by the assistance of many friends and acquaintances. Your assistance came in many ways; some listened, some provided encouragement, some assisted with writing, some provided information and some provided all of the above. Because of you, this book became a reality. For this reason, I extend a heartfelt gratitude to all who gave me support.

Thank you, Doris Madkins, for guiding me to essential biblical scriptures. And, to Janice Baker, who has been with me since the very beginning of W.J. Alexander & Associates: I cherish our friendship and daily am in awe of your patience!

Appreciation also is expressed to the South Texas College of Law Reference Library staff.

Finally, a special thanks to Marsha Tucker, Norma Koontz, Wayne Hall, Marcia West, Troy Taylor, Cynthia Mark, Deanna Slater, William R. Scofield and Ronald Johnson for lending your writing skills. There is no way this book could have been written without you. Whenever the grammar was not quite right, whenever I was searching for the right words or the overwhelming research caused my mind to go blank, you were there.

150

Bibliography

Preface

1. *Diary of Saint Maria Faustina Kowalska, — Divine Mercy in My Soul, pg 490, Notebook V, 1372* – Marian Press – Stockbridge, MA - 2007

2. Pipes, Kasey S., Ike's Final Battle – The Road to Little Rock and the Challenge of Equality, Preface – World Ahead Publishing, Inc., 2007

Prologue

3. National Institute on Drug Abuse, *Monitoring the Future,* Published April 2006

Chapter 1

4. Black Enterprise – July 2001 issue

5. Department of Labor, 1997 U.S. Census Bureau

6. Houston Chronicle article – July 13, 2001

7. US Equal Employment Opportunity Commission, 2005

8. 2002 Economic Census, U.S. Census Bureau, April 2006

9. Houston Chronicle editorial, "Grim Facts" – August 31, 2006

10. Anderson, Claud, Ed.D., *PowerNomics – The National Plan to Empower Black America*, pg 6 — PowerNomics Corporation of America, Inc., 2001

11. Garrow, David J., *Bearing the Cross – Martin Luther King, Jr., And the Southern Christian Leadership Conference*, pg 56-58 - Quill William Morrow, 1986

Chapter 2

12. *A Testament of Hope – The Essential Writings and Speeches of Martin Luther King, Jr.,* pg 279 – Edited by James M. Washington – Harper San Francisco – 1991

13. Robertson, A.T.; M.A., D.D., LL.D., Litt.D., *Events of the Original Lenten Season*

14. Branch, Taylor, *At Canaan's Edge – America in the King Years 1965-68*, pg 10 and 476 — Simon & Schuster, 2006

15. *A Testament of Hope – The Essential Writings and Speeches of Martin Luther King, Jr.,* pgs - pgs 555-567, 619 – Edited by James M. Washington – Harper San Francisco – 1991

Chapter 3

16. Johnson, John L., *The Black Biblical Heritage*, Winston-Derek Publishers, Inc. – 1991 – Library of Congress Cataloging in Publication Data

17. "The Real Eve," Discovery Channel, 2002

18. Holy Bible, King James Version, Family Reference Edition, Thomas Nelson Inc. – 1971

19. Holy Bible, The Life Application Study Bible, Tyndale House Publishers, Inc. – 1996

20. The Oxford English Dictionary — Second Edition - Prepared by J. A. Simpson and E. S. C. Weiner - Clarendon Press — Oxford – 1989

Chapter 4

21. King James Version Hebrew-Greek Key Word Study Bible – AMG Publishers – 1991

Chapter 5

22. Random House Webster's Unabridged Dictionary, Second Edition, Random House, 2001

23. Random House College Dictionary - Revised Edition – 1984

Chapter 6

24. The New Encyclopaedia Britannica — Volume 7, pg 767 – Micropaedia – Ready Reference – Founded in 1768 - 15th

Edition – Encyclopaedia Britannica, Inc. – Jacob E. Safra, Chairman of the Board, Ilan Yeshua, Chief Executive Officer

25. *The Travels of Sir John Mandeville — The Fantastic 14th Century Account of a Journey to the East* – Dover Publications, Inc. — Mineola, New York – 2006

26. Oxford English Dictionary — Second Edition – on CD-ROM Version 3.1 – Oxford University Press - 2004

27. Great World Atlas, pg 121 – Third Edition - A DK Publishing Book -2004

Chapter 8

28. The Oxford English Dictionary — Second Edition - Prepared by J. A. Simpson and E. S. C. Weiner - Clarendon Press — Oxford – 1989

29. National Geographic, pg 61, 62 – March 2006 issue

Chapter 10

30. McCalep Jr., George O., Ph.D., *When Black Men Stretch Their Hands to God / Messages Affirming The Biblical Black Heritage,* Lithonia, Ga., Orman Press, Inc., 2003

Chapter 11

31. Dr. Herbert Lockyer, R.S.L, *All The Women Of The Bible,* pg 162, Grand Rapids, Mich., Zondervan Publishing House, 1991

32. The Holy Bible - New International Version Study Bible – Published by Zondervan, Grand Rapids, Michigan - 2002

Chapter 13

33. Everett, Susanne, *History of Slavery*, pgs 6-7 — Chartwell Books, Inc., 2006

34. Houston Chronicle, May 5, 2006, Opinion Section, Charles Krauthammer article
35. Webster's New World College Dictionary, 4th Edition, IDG Books Worldwide, Inc. -2001
36. Henley, William Ernest, "Invictus"
37. Longfellow, Henry Wadsworth, "A Psalm of Life"

Glossary

Adam – the name of the first man.

abnegation – a giving up of rights, etc.; self-denial

adversity – a condition marked by misfortune, calamity.

allusive - having reference to something implied or inferred.

allusively - (archaic) - symbolically, metaphorically, figuratively.

Amos – a Minor Prophet of the 8th century B.C.; a book of the Bible bearing his name.

ancestor – a person from whom one is descended, esp. one earlier in a family line than a grandparent; forefather; forebear.

ancestral – of or inherited from an ancestor or ancestors.

apostle – a person sent out on a special mission; the first Christian missionary in a place; any of a group of early Christian missionaries; an early advocate or leader of a new principle or movement, especially one aimed at reform.

approach - the method used or steps taken in setting about a task, problem, etc:

appropriate – to take for one's own or exclusive use

archaic - marked by the characteristics of an earlier period; antiquated: an archaic manner; an archaic notion; (of a linguistic form) commonly used in an earlier time but rare in present-day usage except to suggest the older time, as in religious rituals or historical novels.

arduous – requiring great exertion; laborious; difficult.

Aristotle – Greek Aristotles (b. 384 BC, Stagiria, Chalcidice, Greece—d. 322, Chalcis, Euboea), ancient Greek philosopher, scientist, and organizer of research, one of the two greatest intellectual figures produced by the Greeks (the other being Plato).

askew – to one side; crookedly

august – worthy of respect because of age and dignity, high position, etc.

authenticate – to establish the truth of; verify; to prove to be genuine or as represented.

beast – a cruel, coarse, filthy, or otherwise beastlike person. Synonym - barbarian

began - the past tense of "begin" as to start doing, acting, going, etc.; get under way.

beguile – to influence by trickery, flattery, etc.; mislead; delude; to take away from by cheating or deceiving; to charm or divert. To lead astray, to delude, or seduce.

Bevel, James (1936 -) – the charismatic Southern Christian Leadership Conference (SCLC) field general who organized and led many of the actions of the Chicago Freedom Movement. (CivicSpace)

Bible - the collection of sacred writings of the Christian religion, comprising the Old and New Testaments; also called Hebrew Scriptures; the collection of sacred writings of the Jewish religion: known to Christians as the Old Testament. Many books have been written, movies made and stories told of the Holy Bible, the most ancient of documents. To this day, in terms of percentages of the population it is probably the least read and its words are most unknown in the world. One may ask, why is there such a mystery surrounding this sacred book?

Bryant, William Cullen (1794-1878) - U.S. poet & journalist

Brown v. Board of Education – a landmark decision of the United States Supreme Court overturning its earlier ruling, declaring the establishment of separate public schools for black and white students inherently unequal.

Caleb – a Hebrew leader, sent as a spy into the land of Canaan.

Carmichael, Stokely (1941-88) – U.S. civil rights leader, born in Trinidad: chairman of the Student Nonviolent Coordinating Committee 1966-67.

carnal - pertaining to or characterized by the flesh or the body, its passions and appetites, sensual: carnal pleasures; often refers to sexual needs or urges:

cattle – disparaging; human beings, as in "treated like cattle."

CenterPoint Energy - the third largest publicly traded natural gas delivery company in the U.S. with 3 million natural gas customers in six states. They are also the nation's third largest combined electricity and natural gas delivery company, with more than 5 million metered electric and natural gas customers, and the third largest employer in the energy industry in Houston. CenterPoint Energy provides electricity transmission and distribution service for the Houston metropolitan area and natural gas distribution service in Arkansas, Louisiana, Minnesota, Mississippi, Oklahoma and Texas.

chattel – a movable article of personal property.

children of Israel – the Jews; Hebrews

Civil Rights Act of 1964 – To enforce the constitutional right to vote, to confer jurisdiction upon the district courts of the United States to provide injunctive relief against discrimination in public accommodations, to authorize the Attorney General to institute suits to protect constitutional right in public facilities and public education, to extend the Commission on Civil Rights, to prevent discrimination in federally assisted programs, to establish a Commission on Equal Employment Opportunity, and for other purposes.

Civil Rights Movement (1955-1968) – The African-American Civil Rights Movement refers to reform movements in the United States aimed at abolishing racial discrimination of African Americans.

cleave – to remain attached, devoted, or faithful to; † to remain steadfast, stand fast, abide, continue.

Coca-Cola – Markets nearly 2,400 beverage products in more than 200 countries.

cognate – related through the same source; derived from a common original form.

Congress of Racial Equality (CORE) – civil rights organization founded (1942) in Chicago by James Farmer. Dedicated to the use of nonviolent direct action, CORE initially sought to promote better race relations and end racial discrimination in the United States. It first focused on activities directed toward the desegregation of public accommodations in Chicago, later expanding its program of nonviolent sit-ins to the South.

comprehend – to understand the nature or meaning of; grasp with the mind; perceive.

consummate – to make (a marriage) actual by sexual intercourse.

context - the parts of a written or spoken statement that precede or follow a specific word or passage, usually influencing its meaning or effect; the set of circumstances or facts that surround a particular event, situation, etc.

Continental Airlines – a US certificated air carrier. Based in Houston, Texas, it is the fourth-largest airline in the U.S. and the eight-largest in the world by revenue passenger miles.

coveted - to desire wrongfully, inordinately, or without due regard for the rights of others; to have an inordinate or wrongful desire.

confluence – a coming together of people or things.

create – to cause to come into being, as something unique that would not naturally evolve or that is not made by ordinary processes.

credible – that can be believed; believable; reliable

Daniel – a prophet living in Babylon during the Captivity; the book of the Bible bearing his name.

darkness - the state or quality of being dark; absence or deficiency of light; wickedness or evil; obscurity: concealment; lack of knowledge or enlightenment: heathen darkness.

Davis, Ossie (1917-2005) – An African-American actor, writer, producer, and director. (The African American Registry)

decipher – to translate into ordinary, understandable language; decode.

deep – heartfelt; sincere: deep affections; inextricably involved.

delight – a high degree of pleasure or enjoyment; joy; rapture; something that gives great pleasure; to give great pleasure, satisfaction, or enjoyment to; please highly.

delve – to carry on intensive and thorough research for data, information, or the like; investigate.

Department of Labor – is charged with preparing the American workforce with new and better jobs.

derivative – not original; secondary.

derive – to trace from a source or origin.

desired – to desire, covet, long for.

dire – causing or involving great fear or suffering; dreadful; terrible.

discredit – to damage the credit or reputation of; disgrace.

dismal – causing gloom or misery; depressing.

disparage – to speak of or treat slightingly; depreciate; belittle; to bring reproach or discredit upon; lower the estimation of: Synonym – ridicule, discredit, mock, demean, denounce, derogate.

disparity – inequality or difference, as in rank, amount, quality, etc.

diverse – different; dissimilar.

dogma – a doctrine or body of doctrines formally and authoritatively affirmed.

dream – a succession of images, thoughts, or emotions passing through the mind during sleep.

dullard – a stupid, insensitive person.

east – a cardinal [of prime importance] point of the compass, 90 degrees to the right of north.

eastward – moving, bearing, facing, or situated toward the east.

efficacy – capacity for producing a desired result or effect.

Egypt – an ancient kingdom in NE, Africa: divide into the Nile Delta (Lower Egypt) and the area from Cairo South to the Sudan (Upper Egypt).

elaborate – to state something in detail or add more details.

Eleatic – ancient Greek colony in Italy designating or of an ancient Greek school of philosophy which held that true being is singular and unchanging and that plurality, change, and motion are illusory: Parmenides and Zeno were its best-known adherents.

Emancipation Proclamation – a proclamation issued by President Lincoln in September, 1862, effective January 1, 1863, freeing the slaves in all territory still at war with the Union.

emigrate – to leave one country or region to settle in another; migrate. To emigrate is to leave a country, usually one's own (and take up residence in another).

emigrant – a person who emigrates, as from his or her native country or region.

engender – to bring into being; bring about; cause; produce.

enmity – a feeling or condition of hostility; hatred; ill will; animosity; antagonism.

Enron Corp – Enron Corporation was an American energy company based in Houston, Texas. Before its bankruptcy in late 2001, Enron employed around 21,000 people and was one of the world's leading electricity, natural gas, pulp and paper, and communications companies, with claimed revenues of $111 billion in 2000. *Fortune* named Enron "America's most Innovative Company" for six consecutive years. It achieved infamy at the end of 2001, when it was revealed that its reported financial condition was sustained mostly by institutionalized, systematic, and creatively planned accounting fraud. Enron has since become a popular symbol of willful corporate fraud and corruption.

entice – to lead on by exciting desire; allure; inveigle.

essential – absolutely necessary; indispensable.

Ethiopia – an ancient region in NE Africa, bordering on Egypt and the Red Sea; the hot zone below 4,900 feet with both tropical and arid conditions and daytime temperatures ranging from 81° – 122° Farenheit.

evangelical - in, of, or according to the Gospels or the teaching of the New Testament; of those Protestant churches, as the Methodist and Baptist, that emphasize salvation by faith and reject the efficacy of the sacraments and good works alone.

exact – strictly accurate or correct: an exact likeness; an exact description; precise, as opposed to approximate: the exact sum; the exact date; admitting of no deviation, as laws or discipline; strict or rigorous.

expose – to make known, disclose, or reveal (intentions, secrets).

extemporaneous – done, spoken, performed, etc., without special advance preparation.

extra – beyond or more than what is expected or necessary; additional; larger or better than what is usual; something extra or additional.

ExxonMobil – a multi-national American corporation and a direct descendant of John D. Rockefeller's Standard Oil Company, is the largest publicly traded integrated petroleum and natural gas company in the world, formed on November 30, 1999, by the merger of Exxon and Mobil.

Eve – name of the first woman: wife of Adam and progenitor of the human race.

evil – bad, inferior quality; any activity which is contrary to God's will, i.e., an attitude which rejects God's authority; the force in nature that governs and gives rise to wickedness and sin. Synonym. sinful

extramarital – pertaining to sexual relations with someone other than one's spouse.

Exxon Mobil Corporation – a multi-national American corporation. Is the largest publicly traded integrated petroleum and natural gas company in the world, formed on November 30, 1999, by the merger of Exxon and Mobil. Among all private oil companies ExxonMobil ranks 1st in the world in proven oil and gas reserves.

fabricate – to make up (a story, reason, lie, etc.); invent

Fair Housing Act – prohibits housing discrimination on the basis of race, color, religion, sex, disability, familial status, and national origin.

faith – belief that is not based on proof; belief in God or in the doctrines or teachings of religion; belief in anything, as a code of ethics, or the occurrence of a future event; a system of religious belief; the Jewish faith; Christian Theology. The trust in God and in His promises as made through Christ and the Scriptures by which man is justified or saved.

famine – an acute and general shortage of food, or a period of this.

feign – to make a false show of; pretend.

fidelity – faithful devotion to duty or to one's obligations or vows; loyalty; faithfulness

figurative – of the nature of or involving a figure of speech, esp. a metaphor; metaphorical; not literal.

flesh – the physical or animal nature of humankind as distinguished from its moral or spiritual nature: the needs of the flesh; in euphemistic phrases with reference to sexual intercourse.

form – the shape of a thing or person; a body, esp. that of a human being.

Freedom March – an organized march protesting a government's restriction of or lack of support for civil rights, esp. such a march in support of racial integration in the U.S. in the 1960's. [1960-65]

fruit – offspring, progeny; also, an embryo.

Garvey, Marcus (1887-1940) – Jamaican black nationalist leader in the U.S.

genealogy - a record or account of the ancestry and descent of a person, family, group, etc.; the study of family ancestries and histories; descent from an original form or progenitor; lineage; ancestry.

generations – it means descent, family, race, history, birth, generation, origin, lineage, family register, record of the family, pedigree, genealogy. It refers to what is produced or brought into being by someone, and sometimes the results. Usually, it does not include the birth of the individual who started the line of descendants.

genital – of reproduction or the sexual organs.

genitalia – short for genitals.

gentile – of or pertaining to any people not Jewish; Christian, as distinguished from Jewish.

germane – closely or significantly related; relevant; pertinent.

ghetto - any section of a city in which many members of some minority group live, or to which they are restricted as by economic pressure or social discrimination.

good – morally sound or excellent; specifically, virtuous; honest; just; devout; kind; benevolent; sympathetic; generous, etc.

Greater Houston Partnership – Founded in 1989, with a merger of the Houston Chamber of Commerce, the Houston Economic Development Council and the Houston World Trade Center, the Greater Houston Partnership is dedicated to building prosperity throughout the ten-county Houston region.

ground – † c. fig. Of the heart; the divine essence or centre of the individual soul, in which mystic union lies.

Haley, Alex Palmer (1921-1992) – American biographer, scriptwriter, and novelist, whose most famous work is ROOTS, a publishing phenomenon and international bestseller. Haley traced in it his ancestry back to Africa and covered seven American generations, starting from his ancestor, Kunta Kinte.

Henley, William Ernest (1849-1903) - English poet, critic, and editor.

Houston Chronicle – is the largest daily newspaper in Houston, Texas, USA. As of March 2007, it is the ninth largest newspaper in the United States.

Houston Independent School District – located in Houston, Texas, is the largest public school system in Texas and the seventh-largest in the United States.

Houston Oilers – one of the original professional football team franchises in the American Football League (AFL). The AFL was founded in 1959 by businessmen K.S. "Bud" Adams Jr., Lamar Hunt and Ralph Wilson. The first three teams in the AFL were the Houston Oilers, owned by Mr. Adams, the Dallas Texans (present day Kansas City Chiefs) owned by Mr. Hunt and the Buffalo Bills owned by Mr. Wilson. The American Football League merged with the National Football League after the 1969 football season. After the 1996 season, Mr. Adams moved the Houston Oilers franchise from Houston, Texas to Memphis, Tennessee as part of the Oilers eventual relocation to Nashville Tennessee. In 1999, the Oilers franchise name was changed to the Tennessee Titans in conjunction with the opening of the teams' new stadium, in Nashville, the Coliseum.

illegitimate – born of parents not [legally] married to each other; bastard.

image –a physical likeness or representation of a person

immigrant – a person who migrates to another country, usually for permanent residence.

immigrate – to come to a country of which one is not a native, usually for permanent residence.

immoral – not in conformity with the accepted standards of proper sexual behavior; unchaste; lewd.

impregnate – to make pregnant.

impromptu – made or done without previous preparation.

inadvertent – unintentional

incarnate – endowed with a body, especially a human body.

incorporated – to combine or join with something already formed; make part of another thing; include; embody.

incredulous – showing doubt or disbelieve.

indomitable – not easily discouraged, defeated, or subdued; un-yielding; unconquerable.

inextricable - incapable of being disentangled, undone, loosed, or solved.

ingenuity – cleverness or skillfulness of conception or design, as of things, actions, etc.

irrelevant – not relating to the subject.

Israelite – a descendant of Jacob, especially a member of the Hebrew people who inhabited the ancient kingdom of Israel.

Jewish Revolt - Second (AD 132-135), Jewish rebellion against Roman rule in Judaea. The revolt was preceded by years of clashes between Jews and Romans in the area. Finally, in AD 132, the misrule of Tinnius Rufus, the Roman governor of Judaea, combined with the emperor Hadrian's intention to found a roman colony on the site of Jerusalem and his restrictions on Jewish religion freedom and observances, roused the last remnants of Palestinian Jewry to revolt. A bitter struggle ensued. Bar Kokhba (q.v.) became the leader of this second Jewish Revolt; although at first successful, his forces proved no match against the methodical and ruthless tactics of the Roman general Julius Severus. With the fall of Jerusalem and then Bethar, a fortress on the seacoast south of Caesarea, the rebellion was crushed in 135. Jews were thenceforth forbidden to enter Jerusalem.

Jim Crow – traditional discrimination against or segregation of blacks, especially in the United States.

John – the apostle John, believed to be the author of the fourth Gospel, three Epistles, and the book of Revelation.

John Paul II, Pope (1920 – 2005) – born Karol Jozef Wojtyla in Wadowice, Poland. Reigned as the 264th Pope of the Catholic Church and Sovereign of the State of the Vatican City from October 16, 1978, until his death more than 26 years later, making his the second-longest pontificate in modern times after Pius IX who reigned for 31 years.

Joshua – the successor of Moses as leader of the Israelites; a book of the Bible bearing his name.

King, Martin Luther, Jr. – (1929-68) – U.S. clergyman & leader in the civil rights movement: assassinated; U.S. Baptist minister: Nobel peace prize 1964

knowing – be acquainted with a woman (in a sexual way, i.e., sexual intercourse)

language – a body of words and the systems for their use common to a people who are of the same community or nation, the same geographical area, or the same cultural tradition.

layaway – a method of purchasing by which the purchaser reserves an article with a down payment and claims it only after paying the full balance.

legend – a story handed down for generations among a people and popularly believed to have a historical basis, although not verifiable.

legendary – of, based on, or presented in legends; the synonym for legendary is fictitious.

Lincoln, Abraham (1809-65) – 16th president of the U.S. (1861-65): assassinated

Lincoln Memorial – stands at the west end of the National Mall [in Washington D.C.] as a neoclassical monument to the 16th President. The memorial, designed by Henry Bacon, after ancient Greek temples, stands 190 feet long, 119 feet wide, and almost 100 feet high.

literal - in accordance with, involving, or being the primary or strict meaning of the word or words; not figurative or metaphorical: the literal meaning of a word; following the words of the original very closely and exactly; true to fact; not exaggerated; actual or factual: a literal description of conditions; being actually such, without exaggeration or inaccuracy: the literal extermination of a city; (of persons) tending to construe words in the strict sense or in an unimaginative way; matter -of-fact

loom – to rise before the vision with an appearance of great or portentous size.

Longfellow, Henry Wadsworth – (1807-82) U.S. poet

Lost Tribe of Israel – the ten tribes of Israel carried off into Assyrian captivity about 722 B.C.

Lowell, James Russell (1819-91) U.S. poet, essayist, & editor

malevolent – wishing evil or harm to another or others; showing ill will;

malice – desire to inflict injury, harm, or suffering on another, either because of a hostile impulse or out of deep-seated meanness.

malicious – full of, characterized by, or showing malice; malevolent; spiteful; malicious gossip.

man – the human individual as representing the species, without reference to sex; the human race; humankind:

Mandeville, Sir John – died 1372, English compiler of a book of travels.

McKissick, Floyd (1922 -) – He was an African-American civil rights activist and a former National Director of the Congress of Racial Equality (CORE). During the time he became active in CORE, replacing James Farmer as its head in 1966. Under McKissick the organization moved more directly into the Black Power movement, refusing to support Martin Luther King Jr.'s nonviolent policy in northern cities. (The African American Registry)

Medieval Church – The Roman Catholic Church was the single, largest unifying structure in medieval Europe. It touched everyone's life, no matter what their rank or class or where they lived. With the exception of a small number of Jews, everyone in Europe was a Christian during the Middle Ages from the richest king down to the lowest serf.

medievalist – a student of or specialist in medieval history, literature, art, etc.

Mediterranean Sea – large sea surrounded by Europe, Africa, & Asia.

Meredith, James (1933 -   ) – one of the pioneers of the civil rights movement. In 1962 he became the first black student to successfully enroll at the University of Mississippi. In 1966 he led the March Against Fear to protest against voter registration intimidation.

Middle East – those regions between the Far East & the near East: rarely used since WWII 2; area from Afghanistan to Libya, including Arabia, Cyprus, U Asiatic Turkey.

midst – the position of being in the interior of, involved or enveloped in, or surrounded by (something, or a number of things or persons, specified or implied). Now almost exclusively in the phrase in the midst of (formerly also †among the midst of) Among, amid, surrounded by (a number of things or persons; while fully engaged with, 'in the thick of' (occupations, troubles, etc.); during the continuance of (an action or condition).

minority – a racial, religious, ethnic, or political group smaller than and differing from the larger, controlling group in a community, nation, etc.

miscegenation – marriage or cohabitation between a man and woman of different races; interbreeding between members of different races.

miscue – a mistake; error.

mist – † a state of obscurity or uncertainty; an atmosphere of doubt. Obsolete

Montgomery Bus Boycott - a political and social protest campaign started in 1955 in Montgomery, Alabama, intended to oppose the city's policy of racial segregation on its public transit system. The ensuing struggle lasted from December 5, 1955, to December 20, 1956, and led to a United States Supreme Court decision that declared the Alabama and Montgomery laws requiring segregated buses unconstitutional.

Moors – member[s] of a Muslim people of mixed Arab and Berber descent living in NW Africa.

Moses – the Hebrew prophet who led the Israelites out of Egypt and delivered the law during their years of wandering in the wilderness.

Mount Sinai – the mountain in S Sinai, of uncertain identity, on which Moses received the law. Ex 19.

Muhammad, Elijah (Elijah Poole) 1897-1975 – U.S. clergyman: leader of the Black Muslims 1934-75.

multitude - a great number; host; a great number of people gathered together; crowd; throng; the state of character of being many; numerousness; the multitude, the common people; the masses.

mystic – a person who claims to attain, or believes in the possibility of attaining, insight into mysteries transcending ordinary human knowledge, as by direct communication with the divine or immediate intuition in a state of spiritual ecstasy.

naked –exposed

nation – an extensive aggregate of persons, so closely associated with each other by common descent, language, or history, as to form a distinct race or people, usually organized as a separate political state and occupying a definite territory; a number of persons belonging to a particular nation; representatives of any nation; †a country, kingdom; Obs. rare, the peoples of the earth; the population of the earth collectively.

nigger – extremely disparaging and offensive. A contemptuous term used to refer to a black person.

nonchalant – coolly unconcerned, indifferent, or unexcited; casual.

obscuration – the act of obscuring.

obscure – not clear or plain; uncertain; to conceal physically; hide or cover; to make confusing or oblique, as the meaning of a statement.

obstacle – something that obstructs or hinders progress.

onyx – black, esp. a pure or jet black; the common onyx has two opaque layers, of different colors, usually in strong contrast to each other.

palatial – befitting or suitable for a palace; stately; magnificent.

paradox – a statement that seems contradictory, unbelievable, or absurd but that may be true in fact.

paradoxical – seemingly full of contradictions

Parmenides – Fifth century, B.C.: Greek Eleatic philosopher.

Parks, Rosa (1913-2005) – U.S. civil rights activist.

Pentateuch – the first five books of the Bible.

perplexed – full of doubt or uncertainty; puzzled; hard to understand; confusing.

Pharaoh – the title of the kings of ancient Egypt: often used as a proper name in the Bible.

Plato – 427?-347? B.C.; Greek philosopher

plummet – something that weighs down or depresses.

poignant – keenly distressing to the feelings.

Poland – country in EC Europe, on the Baltic Sea: a kingdom in the Middle Ages, it lost autonomy throughout much of its later history until proclaimed an independent republic in 1919.

powerbroker – a person who has power and influence, especially one who operates unofficially or behind the scenes as an intermediary.

prejudge – to pass judgment on prematurely or without sufficient reflection or investigation.

procreate – to beget or generate (offspring); to produce; bring into being; to beget offspring;

profound – marked by intellectual depth; intensely felt.

progenitor – a biologically related ancestor.

Promised Land – Bible, Canaan, promised by God to Abraham and his descendants.

prominent – well known.

promiscuity – ties state, quality, or instance of being promiscuous, especially in sexual relations.

promiscuous – engaging in sexual intercourse indiscriminately or with many persons.

prophet – a person who speaks for God or a deity, or by divine inspiration.

pure - free from anything of a different, inferior, or contaminating kind: free from extraneous matter; of unmixed descent or ancestry:

put – the basic meaning is to put something somewhere; to place in a location.

racism – 1. belief in or doctrine asserting racial differences in character, intelligence, etc. and the superiority of one race over another or others: racist doctrine also, typically, seeks to maintain the supposed purity of a race or the races. 2. any program or practice of racial discrimination, segregation, etc. specifically, such a program or practice that upholds the political or economic domination of one race over another or others. 3. feelings or actions of hatred and bigotry toward a person or persons because of their race.

Reconstruction Era – the period (1865-77) after the Civil War when the states that had seceded were reorganized as part of the Union.

regress – backward movement.

relevant – bearing upon or relating to the matter in hand.

reliable – dependable; trustworthy;

religion – a belief in a divine or superhuman poser or powers to be obeyed and worshiped as the creator(s) and ruler(s) of the universe.

religious – characterized by adherence to religion or a religion; devout; pious; godly.

repugnant – contradictory; inconsistent; distasteful; offensive; disagreeable

revelation – a striking disclosure of something not previously known or realized.

ridicule – speech or action intended to cause contemptuous laughter at a person or thing; derision.

river² - a person who rives

Robeson, Paul - 1898- 1976, U.S. singer & actor.

Roman calendar – the calendar used by the ancient Romans before the Julian calendar: it consisted first of ten months, later twelve.

Rosetta Stone – a tablet of black basalt found in 1799 at Rosetta, a town in Egypt: because it bore parallel inscriptions in Greek and in ancient Egyptian demotic and hieroglyphic characters, it provided a key to the deciphering of ancient Egyptian writing.

rudimentary – a mere beginning, first slight appearance, or undeveloped or imperfect form of something.

ruminate – to turn (something) over in the mind; meditate.

saw – to know.

secular – of or relating to worldly things as distinguished from things relating to church and religion; not sacred or religious.

seduce – to persuade or induce to have sexual intercourse.

seminal – having possibilities of future development; being the first or earliest of something that is later recognized as having been of primary influence.

serpent – normally, the serpent was something evil, dating back to the temptation in the Garden of Eden.

servile – of a slave or slaves; like that of slaves or servants; like or characteristic of a slave; humbly yielding or submissive; cringing; abject. [Archaic] held in slavery; not free

show – medical, the first appearance of blood at the onset of menstruation; a blood-tinged mucous discharge from the vagina that indicates the onset of labor.

shower[2] – a person or thing that shows.

slave – a person who is the property of and wholly subject to another; a bond servant.

slavery – the condition of a slave; bondage. The keeping of slaves as a practice or institution.

sleep - sleep together, to be sexual partners; have a sexual relationship; sleep with, to have sexual relations with; †with allusion to sleeping together; Implying sexual intimacy or cohabitation. Also, with around: to engage in sexual intercourse casually with a variety of partners; to be sexually promiscuous

Southern Christian Leadership Conference (SCLC) – an American civil rights organization. It played a prominent role in the Civil Rights Movement of the 1950s and 1960s. SCLC was closely associated with its first president, Martin Luther King, Jr.

Spartacus – died 71 B.C.; Thracian slave and gladiator in Rome: leader of a slave revolt.

status quo – the state in which the existing state of affairs (at a particular time).

stereotype - an unvarying form or pattern; specifically, a fixed or conventional notion or conception, as of a person, group, idea, etc., held by a number of people, and allowing for no individuality, critical judgment, etc.

stigmatize – to characterize or mark as disgraceful.

Stoic – a member of a Greek school of philosophy founded by Zeno about 308 B.C. holding that all things, properties, relations, etc. are governed by unvarying natural laws, and that the wise man should follow virtue alone, obtained through reason, remaining indifferent to the external world and to passion or emotion.

Stoicism – a school of philosophy in Greco-Roman antiquity that stressed duty and held that, through reason, man can come to regard the universe (both physical and moral) as governed by fate and, despite appearance, as fundamentally rational; that, in the regulation of his, he can thus emulate the grandeur of the calm and order of the universe by learning to accept events with a stern and tranquil mind (apathy) and to achieve a lofty moral worth; and that, in contrast to the Epicurean view, man, as a world citizen, is obliged to play an active role in public affairs.

strategy – a) the science of planning and directing large-scale military operations, specifically (as distinguished from TACTICS) of maneuvering forces into the most advantageous position prior to actual engagement with the enemy b) a plan or action based on this.

strategic – of or having to do with strategy.

Student Nonviolent Coordinating Committee (SNCC) – a U.S. civil-rights organization formed by students and active esp. during the 1960's whose aim was to achieve political and economic equality for blacks through local and regional action groups.

subdue – to bring under mental or emotional control, as by persuasion or intimidation; render submissive; to repress (feelings, impulses, etc.)

subjection – being under the dominion or rule of another person.

sub-Saharan – of, pertaining to, or in Africa south of the Sahara Desert

subterfuge - any plan, action, or device used to hide one's true objective, evade a difficult or unpleasant situation.

subtile – of persons: Clever, dexterous, skilful; Cleverly devised; ingeniously contrived; ingenious; Of persons, animals, their actions, etc.: Crafty, artful, sly, cunning; †Of looks: sly. Obs.

subtle – cunning, wily, or crafty

superstition – a belief or notion, not based on reason or knowledge, in or of the ominous significance of a particular thing, circumstance, occurrence, proceeding, or the like.

Supreme Court – the highest court of the United States.

touch – euphemism; sexual contact.

transgress – to overstep or break (a law, commandment, etc.); go beyond (a limit, boundary, etc.) to break a law or commandment; sin

translate – to turn from one language into another or from a foreign language into one's own:

translation – the rendering of something into another language or into one's own from another language.

treacherous - characterized by faithlessness or readiness to betray trust; traitorous; deceptive, untrustworthy, or unreliable.

tree - a genealogical chart showing the ancestry, descent, and relationship of all members of a family or other genealogical group.

truth – a verified or indisputable fact, proposition, principle, or the like:

tryst – an appointment to meet at a specified time and place, esp. one made secretly by lovers.

turbulent – characterized by, or showing disturbance, disorder, etc. being in a state of agitation or tumult; disturbed.

union – an act of uniting or of being united in marriage or sexual intercourse.

United Negro College Fund – a Fairfax, Virginia-based American philanthropic organization that fundraises college tuition money for African-American students and general scholarship funds for 39 historically black colleges and universities. The UNCF was incorporated on April 25, 1944 by Frederick D. Patterson (then president of what is now Tuskegee University), Mary McLeod Bethune, and others.

United States Census Bureau – a division of the United States Department of Commerce, the US Census Bureau is responsible for collecting and providing relevant data about the people and economy of the United States.

United States Department of Commerce – the Cabinet department of the United States government concerned with promoting economic growth.

United States Department of Labor – is charged with preparing the US workforce with new and better jobs

The United States Equal Employment Commission - the agency of the United States Government that enforces the federal employment discrimination laws.

Voting Rights Act of 1965 – This law ended the requirement that would-be voters in the United States take literacy tests to qualify to register to vote, and it provided for federal registration of voters in areas that had less than 50% of eligible minority voters registered.

whole – containing all the elements or parts; entire; complete; constituting the entire amount, extent, number, etc.

without - outside (or out of) the place mentioned or implied; esp. outside the house or room;

wily - full of, marked by, or proceeding from wiles; crafty; cunning.

Young, Andrew Jackson, Jr. (1932-) – African-American leader, clergyman, and public official, b. New Orleans. He was a leading civil-rights activist in the 1960s and, as a Democrat from Georgia, served (1973-77) in the U.S. House of Representatives.

Zeno of Citium - (b. c. 335 BC, Citium, Cyprus—d. c. 263, Athens), Greek thinker who founded the Stoic school of philosophy, which influenced the development of philosophical and ethical thought in Hellenistic and Roman times.

Index

Ruth, (Holy Bible, the Bible
   Book of), 99-100, 105,
   112, 141

-S-

Sahara Desert, 120, 130
Samson, 135, 138
Sarah (Sarai) (wife of
Abraham/Abram), 77, 102, 108,
   141
Satan, 144-146
Selma to Montgomery March,
   27
Seth, 101
Shelah (son of Judah), 103
Shem (son of Noah), 81-83,
   89-91, 96, 105, 107-110,
   116, 119
Sinai Peninsula, 75
Slaves, 23, 27, 31, 42, 102-103,
   111-112, 117-120, 126-130,
   146
Slavery, 3, 23, 29, 31-32,40,
   88, 98, 111, 115-117, 120,
   127-130
Solomon (son of King David),

105, 135
South Lincoln Terrace, 21
Southern Christian Leadership
   Conference (SCLC), 30,
Spartacus, 117, 175
Speranza, Sister, iv
Stampp, Kenneth, 126
Steiner, Mark E., 49
St. Louis, Missouri, 77
Stoics, 117
Student Nonviolent Coordinat-
   ing Committee (SNCC), 29
Sub-Sahara(n) Africa, 40, 43
   83, 116-118
Supreme Court, 86

-T-

Tamar, (Canaanite ancestor of
   Jesus), 81-82, 99-100, 103-
   112, 114, 135
Ten Commandments, 60
Tennessee, 22, 77, 122
Thomas (Jesus' disciple), 41
(Three) Wise Men, 75
Till, Emmett, 127
Timnah, 103